LINCOLN CHRISTIAN COLLEGE AND SEMINARY

P9-DEA-088

TAKE MY HAND

## Other Books by Sharon Marshall

# SHARON MARSHALL

## *with* JEFF JOHNSON

# TAKE MY HAND

### GUIDING YOUR CHILD THROUGH GRIEF

**ZONDERVAN™**

GRAND RAPIDS, MICHIGAN 49530

# ZONDERVAN™

*Take My Hand*
Copyright © 2001 by Sharon Marshall

Requests for information should be addressed to:

Zondervan, *Grand Rapids, Michigan 49530*

**Library of Congress Cataloging-in-Publication Data**

Marshall, Sharon, 1943–
    Take my hand : guiding your child through grief / Sharon Marshall
with Jeff Johnson.
       p. cm.
    Includes bibliographical references.
    ISBN 0-310-23845-5
    1. Children—Religious life.   2. Bereavement in children—Religious
aspects—Christianity.   3. Death—Religious aspects—Christianity.   I.
Johnson, Jeff, 1973–   II. Title.
    BV4571.2 .M32 2001
    248.8'66—dc21
                                 2001026968

All Scripture quotations, unless otherwise indicated, are taken from the *Holy Bible: New International Version*®. NIV®. Copyright © 1973, 1978, 1984 by International Bible Society. Used by permission of Zondervan. All rights reserved.

All rights reserved. No part of this publication may be reproduced, stored in a retrieval system, or transmitted in any form or by any means—electronic, mechanical, photocopy, recording, or any other—except for brief quotations in printed reviews, without the prior permission of the publisher.

*Interior design by Beth Shagene*

*Printed in the United States of America*

01 02 03 04 05 06 07 08 /❖ DC/ 10 9 8 7 6 5 4 3 2 1

*From Sharon:*
This book is my loving tribute to its subjects,
My two sons:

Jeff, my firstborn, my coauthor;
The son I got to raise on earth.
You continue to bring me joy and make me proud.

Justin, my son who was raised in heaven.
Heaven is only a memory away.
You taught me that love transcends time and space.
Once I understood the bond between mother and child,
I could begin to comprehend
The love of God.

*From Jeff:*
To the four cutest kids I've ever seen in my entire life:
Breanne, Andrew, Alyssa, and Cambria,
My "adopted" nieces and nephew.
I love you very much.

101605

101603

# Contents

# Preface

We don't like to think of death, especially that of a young child or that which directly affects a young child's life. Yet it is a fact of our lives, and when death shatters the world of a child, we need strategies to help that child grow and cope. Heartaches must be weathered and mourned. Until they are mourned in a healthy way, they will be expressed in unhealthy behaviors. But when loss strikes our family, our children need us at a time when we are caught up in our own mourning and feel least able to help.

I became interested in this topic out of necessity; few study death before it strikes. By the time my son was four, four close family members had entered eternity. The third death was our Justin, Jeff's infant brother, and we had just spent nine months preparing Jeff for his sibling's birth. My own mourning was difficult. I realize now that my ignorance of the grief process and of techniques for teaching children about the fragility of life on earth and about the reality of life hereafter made mourning more difficult for my toddler than it would have been had I only been equipped to help him.

Justin was born hydrocephalic. We had no warning of a problem prior to delivery. The hospital, the doctors, and our friends were very wonderful. We received tender, loving care as we walked through our trauma. We got wise advice: "This is a heaven baby.

Love him while you can." We also heard impossible suggestions: "Go home and forget you ever had him and have another one." Whether the advice was wise or terrible, it was given in love. Love is always the balm that heals.

Justin only lived four and a half months. About half his life was spent in the hospital; he had five brain surgeries. Our hopes could soar or plummet in a moment as we heard the conflicting reports: "Anything's possible; he could live all his life in a vegetative state, or he could be a normal child."

> *If you are reading this book, you probably love a child whose heart is broken.*

How do we usher our children through such grief and loss? When tragedy strikes, to send them away or try to help them forget builds in them a pattern of escapism. Attempting to comfort them by sharing our faith sometimes brings confusion; those things we know about heaven are not understood by a small child. They haven't figured out yet that Jesus doesn't have skin and that we can't fly to heaven in an airplane.

*Take My Hand* addresses these issues of grief as they relate to children. Each part follows a theme; each chapter is short and focused, beginning with a true-story illustration and containing guidance for bereaved and hurting families. Each chapter has a coda written by my son Jeff, now an adult sociologist. Jeff works in a nonpublic school with children who for various reasons are not able to manage a public school experience. Some live with parents or foster parents; some live in a residential setting. His experience adds a unique perspective to the topic of each chapter. His Christian faith, memories, and words of encouragement also serve as a vivid reminder that God heals and that he grows goodness wherever he finds a willing heart.

**Part 1** discusses tough lessons about life. Its six chapters help us distinguish the difference between what is true and what is not as we come face to face with our beliefs (and those of our well-meaning loved ones) about how a child perceives death. It includes those things we've all heard, such as "Troubles come in bundles," and those things we know but find hard to face, such as "It will affect them."

**Part 2** addresses the tough questions parents suddenly find themselves asking: "Should I cry in front of my children?" "How do I talk about it?" "Are they old enough to attend services?"

**Part 3** offers responses to questions young children typically ask, ad infinitum: "Where is heaven?" "When can I go to heaven?" "What happens when you die?"

**Part 4** reveals tough questions children don't usually ask. Sometimes they are not sophisticated enough to even know the questions are there, but the questions come out in unexplained illnesses, fears, and changes in behavior: "Did I cause this?" "If I get sick, will I die, too?" "Will you die and leave me, too?"

**Part 5** poses the ultimate question, the question that haunts the minds of both parents and children, the question that doesn't really have an answer but the one we all cry out when grief strikes: "Why would a good God let this happen?"

"Afterthoughts" offers pearls of wisdom gleaned from the chapters, helping us create a philosophy of life, parenting, and suffering.

A resource section at the end of the book guides you in finding support in your area.

If you are reading this book, you probably love a child whose heart is broken. Anticipating his or her pain is, in many ways, worse than bearing your own. Be encouraged that as you take your child's hand on this journey, you will discover healing and hope.

I offer my heartfelt sympathy. I pray these pages will give you guidance. I *know* God's love can bring you peace.

# Part 1

## Tough Lessons About Life ... and Death

*D*on't cry, Mommy! Justin's in heaven. He's all better. He doesn't hurt any-more. He's with Jesus. Please don't cry, Mommy!"

*We had done what most parents in such circumstances do—we had intel-lectualized death for our young child, in an effort to keep him from feeling its sting. Now we had to teach him that it was okay to cry, and we all had to learn to bear our sorrow together.*

*How would our three-year-old Jeff cope with the death of his baby brother?*

*Some told us he wouldn't remember.*

*Some advised us to protect him from death's reality by sending him to visit a relative or friend until the flurry had subsided.*

*Many people reminded us that he would need an extra dose of love and attention, given the new reality of our lives.*

*Some encouraged us to include him in the mechanics and ceremonials of burial.*

*Some said that the best thing we could do for him was to help him forget.*

Every child will react differently to loss, and every child has a unique capacity to understand and express feelings. Children, though, like adults, must learn to deal with life's hurts, or heartaches will shadow the rest of their lives.

> *Children, like adults, must learn to deal with life's hurts, or heartaches will shadow the rest of their lives.*

Jeff's reaction to Justin's death was keen because death itself was no stranger. There had been two other deaths in our immediate family within recent months. All children have similar characteristics, however, and understanding childlike qualities in light of death will help parents to help their children grow when they face life's major disappointments.

One of the most difficult decisions that faces us when death invades our world is, what do we tell our children?

Tell children the truth:

- Grandpa is not sleeping; he died. If we tell them Grandpa is sleeping, they will be afraid to go to sleep.
- Auntie Jo didn't go away; she is dead. If we tell them she went away, they will be afraid to visit their friends for fear that they too can never come back. They might feel abandoned by their beloved Auntie Jo.
- Little Susie didn't die because the good die young. She died because she was hit by a car. If we tell them the good die young, they will want to be naughty so they won't to die.
- Baby Justin isn't singing with the angels. Well, then again, maybe he is, but when a small child considers this, he interprets it literally. He thinks we can visit and listen to Justin singing in the angel choir. We need to reiterate: Baby Justin is in heaven with Jesus. He died. We're sad and we miss him.

We'll miss him always. It's okay—in fact, it's normal—to cry when we miss him. But life will go on and it will be good. And someday when it's our turn to die, we will see him again. We live for Jesus, and we will go to heaven when we die, too. After we get there, no one will ever be sick or die again. Baby Justin is all well now. Even though we miss him, we are happy he doesn't hurt anymore. We want to live and enjoy life—and we look forward to heaven when we die. Then we will see your brother again.

*If we are to talk with our children honestly, we must feel our own emotional pain.*

One of the many reasons why telling children about death is so difficult is that we must confront our own mortality and perhaps our lack of faith. Also, if we are to talk with our children honestly, we must feel our own emotional pain. Some of us do not talk freely about our emotions. Perhaps we've never been comfortable crying in front of someone else. If we are to help our children, we must also get help for ourselves.

We've heard the clichés all our lives:

- Life's not fair.
- Troubles come in bundles.
- Why do bad things happen to good people?

They seem so trite, yet on the threshold of death we are thrust face to face with our preconceived notions about what is true and what is not. How do we sort through our own untested theories and all the well-intended advice of loved ones and find the true, honest lessons that we and our grieving children need to learn to emerge from this time of loss stronger, wiser, and whole?

———————

*I remember comforting my mom when I was probably seven or eight. She was sitting in her room crying, and I came in and sat next to her and put my arms around her and told her I loved her. After a few minutes of silence together, she stopped crying. So I said, "Hey, I should come hug you every time you cry, because that will help you stop." My goal was to make my mom not sad anymore. It seems to be inherent in everyone, even young children, that when we see sadness, we do whatever we can to make it go away and to get back to the happy times. I mean, hey, who wants to see his or her mommy sad? I think by this time I realized it was okay to miss Justin and that missing him was what made us sad.*

*I can remember my mother teaching me, when I was three, that heaven was this wonderful place where everyone was healed from their earthly afflictions. She told me this was the place where my brother had gone. At that age I didn't quite understand the impact of death and how it affected those left behind. All I knew was that my mom was the smartest person ever and had answers to everything. So if she told me everyone got better in heaven, then that meant my brother Justin too. And if he was better, then we had no reason to cry or be sad. We should, in my young mind, act just the opposite and be happy that Justin was no longer suffering.*

*Three-year-olds have this way of seeing everything in black and white and believing that their parents are always right. For this reason I feel we can be brutally honest with children. They call things the way they see them, as either being fair or unfair, right or wrong. We adults need to do the same when helping children deal with life and death.*

*Chapter 1*

# It Will Affect Them

*We're praying Justin's handicap won't affect Jeff."*

*"Then I guess you had better quit praying."*

*Stunned by these words from a friend—in fact, horrified by them—I, who am never without words, was speechless. When my friend felt the pain of my silence, he explained, "If a normal child had been born into your home, it would affect Jeff. To pray that the handicap won't affect him is to pray the prayer of denial. It will affect him. Begin now to pray instead that this event, the handicap [and eventual death] of his brother, will serve as an influence for good and not for evil."*

*I've thanked my friend (who is also a professor in rehabilitation counseling) many times for his words of wisdom. That year in our lives is still like a black cloud in my memory, so pronounced it was with sorrow. This conversation began my journey to walk in truth, no matter what happened.*

---

We can't have emotional health without truth. We laud truth, but when tragedy strikes, we simply cannot comprehend or admit the truth of our situation all at once. God has equipped us with an intuitive gift; grief counselors call it shock and denial. It eases us into our new reality and gives us the strength to get through the mechanics of ceremony and burial. If we get stuck here and don't move on, our loss haunts us for the rest of our lives. If we work through our pain and cry our tears, our loved one remains a cherished memory—and the experience of walking through our grief will enrich us with new strength and endurance for the future.

*Recognize reactive behaviors as childish versions of our own grief.*

A child unaffected by the death of a loved one is a myth. When we see children playing, seemingly unaware of the pain of loss, they, like adults, are in the grief stage of shock and denial. It will take a while for them to understand what has happened and learn to assimilate death into their conscious minds.

Moving from shock and denial to acceptance is not an easy journey. We have a slogan in our grief recovery classes:

It is true that the truth sets you free.
But before it does, it gives you a whole bunch of pain!

## How Can We Tell That Our Children Are Grieving?

Look for changes or extremes in their behavior:

Did they color within the lines, but now they scribble?
Has the content or style of their drawing changed?
Are they spending more or less time alone than before?
Has their frustration level heightened?
Are they more shy or more talkative than they were before?
Have they become clingy or withdrawn?
Have their eating habits changed?
Has their sense of humor changed?
Have they developed new illnesses or fears?
Are they afraid to go to sleep?

Are they more childish or more mature than is normal for
their age?

These are normal reactions. As we observe them, we should
encourage our children to talk, listen to them, hold them, read
to them, and call them when we are away for extended periods
of time. We might occasionally suggest an emotion: "Are you sad
that Uncle John died?"

This is not the time to scold or correct our children for the
reactive behaviors listed above, unless of course their behavior is
harmful. In fact, we shouldn't even voice our concerns to them.
Instead we should overdose them with love and affection. Life as
they knew it has been dealt a mortal blow. Recognize these behaviors as childish versions of our own grief. I remember, for example, a period of time after Justin died when the ring of a
telephone could send me into a panic attack. It had so often been
the bearer of bad news that I had a conditioned response. These
reactions are not signs of crisis; they are signs of fear because of
a broken heart.

In times of sorrow we parents are wonderful mother hens. We
want to gather our children together, tuck them under our wings,
and shield them from the harsh realities of
life. We want to protect them from the ugli-
ness and sorrow of the pain in the world
around them. It is so much easier to bear grief
ourselves than to allow our children to experience it. Yet experience it they must. No matter what we do, no matter what we say, life
with its heartaches and joys will happen to
them. When we accept that truth, our role can switch from protecting them to mentoring them.

> *Teach children
> how to deal with
> rather than repress
> their anger.*

## What Can We Do or Say?

Watching and wondering is so difficult! Sometimes we learn to pray as parents not because we have great faith and not because we are righteous. Sometimes we pray because we have no alternative. Name each of your children daily in prayer. Do this every day of their lives, in good times and in bad. Whether you believe in prayer or not, I promise it will change your life.

But we can and should do more than pray. In the wake of grief you might try the following:

Encourage your children to talk about the deceased.
Encourage your children to cry when they need to.
Cry with them when you need to.
Teach them how to deal with rather than repress their
   anger.

Encourage them to express their thoughts, fears, and feelings creatively:

Draw a picture of Grandpa.
Sing a song about Mary.
Write a letter to Dad; ask Jesus to make sure he gets it.
Write a book about Grandma.
Tell me again how you and Stevie saved that kitten.
Tell Fido (or Dolly) about Justin.
Help me remember what he looked like.
Talk to God about Aunt Emily.

Allow your children to live a normal life:

Have them invite friends over.
Let them spend the night with friends.
Talk about it when they need to.

Don't talk about it if they don't want to.
Play with them; laugh with them; read to them; pray with
     them.
Hug them.
Laugh with them again.
Hug them some more.

## How Long Will Grieving Take?

Psychologists teach that two years is the normal grieving time. In reality every person is different. For some the loved one quickly becomes a cherished memory; for others the pain is carried a lifetime. It depends on so many factors. My experience is that Jeff is always about two years behind me in facing his pain. About two years after I conquered my own fears and began to face life, Jeff was able to work through his fears. About two years after I quit being embarrassed about the divorce that followed Justin's death, Jeff began to confront his embarrassment about being from a broken home. About two years

*When sadness replaces our anger, embarrassment, or fear, we are coming to terms with our loss.*

after I finally got honest with God about my anger, Jeff faced his anger for the first time.

According to psychologist Phil Southerland, the resolution of grief is sadness.[1] This means that when sadness replaces our anger, embarrassment, or fear, we are coming to terms with our loss. As our lives progress, however, it is normal to relive our experience, merging our adult knowledge with our earlier emotional understanding and allowing Jesus to comfort us in the midst of our pain.

In children this means every new situation could trigger their grief. If they have learned healthy ways to handle stress, their grief will be expressed:

"Let's invite Grandma to my birthday party."
"But I want her *here* for Christmas." [Translated, "I'm tired of this heaven stuff!"]
"I wonder what Mom would have thought about that."
"Boy, Gramps would have had fun with this one!"

In Bob Benson's wonderful book *Come Share the Being*, he captures this sentiment in discussing the grief we experience when our children leave home:

> *And I was thinking about God*
> *He sure has plenty of children*
> *plenty of artists,*
> *plenty of singers,*
> *and carpenters,*
> *and candlestick makers,*
> *and preachers,*
> *plenty of everybody . . .*
> *except you*
> *and all of them together can never*
>     *take your place.*
> *And there will always be*
> *an empty spot in His heart*
> *and a vacant chair at His table*
> *when you're not home.*[2]

Grief isn't something we get over. It is something we get through. Our loss will always be a fact of our lives; it will always be a part of our children's heritage. It becomes a new color in the tapestry that makes us who we are.

## When Do Our Children Need Extra Help?

Grief reactions can become problematic. If grief is too painful, or if showing grief is considered inappropriate in our home, we can't express our heartache in healthy ways, so we repress it. When this happens, we enter what is called the sleeper effect of grief; it is buried very much alive, and it clouds everything we do.

How can we tell our children are mourning? By watching their behavior. Any major change in behavior that lasts longer than a typical mood swing is a sign that something is seriously wrong. Professionally, I am founder and director of SCORE, a nationally validated program for getting at-risk students turned on to learning, mastering their course content, and graduating eligible for college or career. I train school staff to watch grades. If a student's grade moves from A to C or lower in one class, that student needs our help to deal with a teacher conflict or a difficult subject. If a student's grades drop across the board, that student is in crisis and needs intervention. It's that simple. The crises differ from one situation to the next, but the principle never fails.

*Any major change in behavior that lasts longer than a typical mood swing is a sign that something is seriously wrong.*

The following are signs of deeper grief. They too are normal once in a while. If they last beyond a few incidents, you may need to look for help outside your immediate family (see the "Resources" section at the end of the book).

Drawings obsessed with death or violence
Cruelty to other children (beyond age-appropriate spats)
Cruelty to animals
Phantom or copycat illnesses
Facial tics or body twitches
Eyes that periodically cross or won't focus
Obsessive behavior
Lethargy or hyperactivity
Extreme behaviors inappropriate for the child's age
No reaction at all, as though the death didn't matter

When heartache and brokenness, the uninvited guests, visit our home, they will affect our children. If we pray that they will serve as an influence for good rather than evil, we are moved into action. We must look for the good that God has promised will come, rather than bemoaning the helplessness of the situation or pretending it doesn't hurt. God has not promised us that everything that happens to us will be good, but he has promised us that he is bigger than our every circumstance and that he has the power to grow good from our life's ashes of grief.

> *Grief isn't something we get over. It is something we get through.*

> We know that in all things God works for the good of those who love him, who have been called according to his purpose.
>
> ROMANS 8:28

About two years after I wrote my book *Justin, Heaven's Baby,* my son Jeff wrote a book. He was about eight when he wrote this, but it sounds emotionally like the three-year-old he was when Justin died.

## My Brother Is Going to Die

BY JEFF JOHNSON

He died two days ago.

You should have seen my brother before he died. My family misses him very much. We love him very much. He was the nicest brother I've ever had in my entire life. I wish he was still here.

I used to play with him very much. One time I asked him, "Let's go play football." I bet you guys are going to laugh at this. Please don't laugh at me. I will miss him very much. So will my mom and dad. We love him very, very, very much. We wish he was still alive.

He was in the hospital for two and a half months. I got to hold him in the hospital. I was only three years old then. Sometimes I cry nowadays. We wish he was alive. When he died, he was four and a half months old.

I knew he was going to die soon. He was the nicest brother I ever had. We miss him very much. My mom said, "He is very sick. He will die soon." We miss him, and he misses us.

———————

*I have always had an extra sense of compassion for those struggling in life, and I don't know quite how to explain it. I have been dramatically affected by my brother, even though I don't remember consciously deciding to make his death a positive part of my life. I was only three when Justin died; I didn't know about my mother's conversation or her prayer that his death would serve as an influence for good in my life, but her prayers were certainly answered. I never remember a time when I was bitter over my brother—I was just lonely for him.*

*I think my brother's handicap has made me much more aware today of how the disabled need help. I seem to have the necessary patience to work with those who are less able than I am, and I really enjoy it. I know that it's easy for me to talk to handicapped people.*

*I always see some part of Justin when I come across children with disabilities. A child where I work has a shunt in his head because of hydrocephalus (the disease that afflicted Justin). I think it is much easier for me to understand and care for him after having gone through the trauma and grief of my brother's handicap and death. Had I not gone through this, I would not have known to treat this young boy with dignity rather than pity or fear. I laugh with him, talk with him, tease him, play with him. God is able to work in my life and through Justin's to give me compassion and confidence.*

*Children learn how to cope with challenges by observing the behavior of others.*

*Encourage children to write out what they think. I don't remember writing that little passage, but it helps me see what I was thinking about and how I was dealing with Justin and his death. I missed getting to have someone to play with, be a brother to. I didn't have a little brother to boss around anymore. Those who have siblings can appreciate that.*

*The fact that I was about two years behind my mother in dealing with things is quite normal. Children learn how to cope with challenges by observing the behavior of others. It wasn't until I saw my mom come to grips with the reality of loss and make it a healthy part of her life that I could know how to do the same.*

## Chapter 2

# Most People Can't Talk About It

*We were the only two customers amid six beauticians that night. One was working on my hair; five were being entertained by my gregarious, talkative four-year-old, Jeff. They had gathered around the chair he occupied and were laughing at his antics.*

*Then came such a natural, innocent question: "How many brothers and sisters do you have?"*

*And he responded enthusiastically, "I have one brother. He's in heaven!"*

*The woman working on my hair grew silent. The five who had been playing with Jeff openly gasped; every one of them dropped what they were doing and walked out of the room without uttering another word.*

---

One of the toughest parts of watching children grieve is distinguishing between their natural curiosity and their pain. They so innocently and excitedly talk about who they have lost. They don't understand yet the emotional pain that comes when goodbye is forever in terms of our earthly life; they think the dead person is just gone for a while. Occasionally people will talk with them. More often, however, people become quiet or suddenly disappear, as in the above scenario. When this happens, children take it personally.

My own dilemma was so much deeper. I didn't know how to shield Jeff from emotional pain in times like these. I asked myself, *Do I tell my son not to talk about Justin? Do I try to make him understand that people don't know how to respond when we talk about sad things? Can he distinguish between feeling sad that Justin is gone and being happy that he is now whole and pain-free in heaven? Can he understand that both good and bad emotions can coexist, and that's okay?*

## Why Are People Reluctant to Talk About the Deceased?

We adults are uncomfortable in the midst of another person's pain. The parent in us wants to stop the flow of tears or correct the words we hear. We adults enjoy a good party when we are together, but we like to cry alone.

Perhaps we don't talk about the deceased because sometimes God gives us an uncanny peace and we don't have to walk through the usual grief process. The God who created the mourning process is also the God of exceptions.

But perhaps we are reluctant to talk because we assume that those who have real faith will always be delivered from overwhelming sorrow. We preach this philosophy as truth to others. We believe it, too—believe, that is, until death knocks at our own door. Guilt then comes uninvited and is often denied as we seek to resolve our feelings of hurt, disappointment, and sorrow in relationship to God's will and our humanity. In these instances if we talked, we would have to express anger at God or admit feeling that the very God in whom we have placed our trust has let us down.

Perhaps we can't talk about death because we have a tendency to place life's truly hurtful experiences into a small corner of our memory, in a box labeled "Do not open." When we speak of these experiences, then, we only remember the good things that happened as a result, and our personal growth. Thus our role models advise us to hold on and keep trusting, but fail to tell us that a struggle is normal and that rain is usually the price one must pay for sunshine.

Perhaps we are reluctant to speak of death because we have read of the God of miracles and expect him to act for us exactly as he did at times in Scripture. We want instant healing resulting from a touch of God. In translating that fact into real life, however, we box in the God who created variety. Then when God chooses to show his power and fulfill his promises through the death of one we love, we must seek excuses and rationalizations in order to justify the God of our expectations.

Perhaps we don't like to talk about death because we listen to glowing accounts of God's sustaining power during the initial crisis, at the funeral, and when our friends are in the grief stage of shock and denial, but we don't see those same people after the funeral or in their lonely hours as they walk through the other stages of the normal grieving process.

Perhaps we are reluctant to talk about it because

- we fear it will make others sad.
- we think that if we cry in front of others, it will make them feel worse.
- we don't know what to say, so it's easier to say nothing.
- we have our own repressed grief, and talking will open a door we may not be able to shut.
- if we talk about it, we must face the fact that we too are mortal.

## Why Is It Dangerous Not to Talk about Death?

If we don't express our grief in healthy ways, our grief and tears and anger go inside us. Repressed anger becomes depression. Depression may eventually become suicide. Repressed grief may be expressed physically through ulcers, hives, high blood pressure, heart palpitations, and other stress-related diseases. It may be expressed emotionally through overreactions to minor infractions; an example of this is road rage. Many unfulfilling relationships occur because we are so afraid of being abandoned or rejected yet again when we honestly share our hopes, dreams, fears, shortcomings, and heartaches. When we don't share at a heart level, intimacy is impossible. Without intimacy, fulfilling relationships are impossible. When we see destructive patterns in our relationships, it may be because we have not resolved a past grief experience. Dick Innes, director of Acts, International, says it this way: "Every unshed tear is a prism through which the rest of life's heartaches are distorted."[3]

*Repressed anger becomes depression.*

## What Should We Teach Our Children?

We should teach our children that

- tears are a natural, normal way to express grief.
- talking about the deceased is a good way to help us feel and eventually let go of our pain.
- talking about the deceased is a healthy way to help us remember.
- although some people are uncomfortable when we talk about a loved one who died, many people will understand.

- we don't need to be ashamed of our tears; they are our friends because they help us get rid of bad and sad feelings.

It is important to help our children find people to talk with (aunts, siblings, grandparents, counselors, Sunday school teachers, etc.), because their grief is so intertwined with ours that we aren't always safe listeners.

After the beauty shop incident, I wondered if I should speak to Jeff about not talking in front of people about Justin. I thought perhaps I should tell him it was inappropriate in public settings. I debated whether I should teach him only to talk with Jesus and me, so he wouldn't make other people uncomfortable.

Then I realized a great truth. The world will teach him the tough lessons about burying grief. I need to be the person who teaches him to express it. I need to be the one who teaches him to feel rather than repress his emotions. I need to teach him it is okay to cry, even if the whole world doesn't understand. I need to let him know that the only stupid thing about questions is not asking them. I need to help him cherish the memory of his brother rather than stifle his pain.

> ✠ *The world will teach my child the tough lessons about burying grief. I need to be the person who teaches him to express it.* ✠

---

*Talking with people about death is a strange thing. People either empathize for a couple of minutes with you, or they shut down and leave. Just recently I was talking with an acquaintance about the death of my best friend's mother, and she suddenly made an excuse to leave the room. People don't like feeling pain and want to do what they can to remain happy, so their natural reaction when the* topic of death is brought up is to leave or try to change the subject to the happy things of life.

The children I work with don't understand why they feel the way they do. They have no real skills to identify the reason why they are angry or hurting; they just know they are. No one has taught them how to name their emotional pain or given them permission to feel it. As a result, they grow up never wanting to face the pain in their lives, because they never learned an appropriate way to deal with it.

Three-year-olds are naturally curious and very honest in their responses. So the way I answered the beauticians is typical. I was telling the truth: I have a brother but he's dead. In my young mind that's all I needed to know.

I think it's always tough at first to teach children that it's okay to remember bad things like death. It's normal to want to keep children from experiencing pain in any form, but in the long run, not allowing your children to talk it out and feel the hurt initially will result in more pain years later. If you let your children feel hurt, it will allow them to be more honest with themselves and help them understand how to cope. It will also help them know better how to support grieving friends later in life.

## Chapter 3

# Troubles Come in Bundles

*O*ne morning I just couldn't face the day. I had to get away. I piled Jeff in the car and went to the park. We didn't tell anyone where we were going. When I arrived home after dinner, the phone was ringing. My family had been trying to reach me all day with the news that my stepfather had passed away. His was our fourth family death in what I still refer to as the year of the big black cloud. My sister Velda was packed and impatiently waiting for me to go to our mother.

All my clothes were dirty, waiting for me to summon the energy to do the laundry. We had a four-hour drive ahead of us, and already my absence had delayed our trek. My silence had caused them to worry about me, too, adding stress to an event that was already laden with tension. I stuffed my dirty clothes into a plastic bag and headed out.

As was typical of that awful year, we had car trouble en route. We called other family members to stay with our mother, and we arrived at an aunt's house about 3:00 A.M.

Early the next morning I threw my dirty clothes into her washer and threw Jeff into the shower, eager to get to my mother. As I dried him off, I found bumps—little welts—all over his body.

Since we were away from home, I took Jeff to the emergency room to verify that these were indeed the signs of chicken pox. The long delay at the emergency room was probably God's gift of mercy to my mother. She didn't need me and my problems at her side just then!

*I paced, badgered the receptionist to get me in sooner, and complained loudly. An intern walked by as I once again said to the receptionist, "All I need to know is, does he have chicken pox?"*

*The intern replied, "Bring him here. I can tell you if it's chicken pox."*

*I held Jeff up to the window; he peered at the welts and pronounced, "Yup, that's chicken pox, all right!"*

*To which I replied frantically, "Well, what do I do with the chicken pox?"*

*The intern looked at me, shook his head, and responded, "You give him Tylenol if he runs a fever and keep him quiet. And then, lady, you go home and have a shot of whiskey. You're in a lot worse shape than he is!"*

----

Jeff was born into a happy family. He was our hearts' delight. We were blessed with a loving extended family. Then his world began to change.

Living through our crises, I thought they would consume me and destroy him, but we made it through somehow. Today life is victorious for both Jeff and me. It is not the life we had planned, but it is good.

Troubles do often come in bundles. Those old sayings usually stem from at least a grain of truth.

> The year I was pregnant with Justin, my mother-in-law died after a long, tough bout with lymphoma.
>
> Justin was born hydrocephalic, underwent a series of brain surgeries, and died four and a half months later.
>
> My grandfather, who had raised me, died during Justin's short lifetime.
>
> My stepfather died shortly after Justin's death.
>
> One month after we buried our son, my husband, a recovering alcoholic, hit the bars and never returned. Another

tragedy followed the one we had just witnessed—the tragedy of divorce. I lost my home and virtually everything I owned. Jeff and I started over, just the two of us, supported by a host of family and friends.

I was so broken over the senseless divorce that a therapist had to help me mourn the loss of my son. I am so grateful he did. My grief work resulted in the publication of *Justin, Heaven's Baby.* The process of writing that book and crying a mountain of tears transformed Justin from my life's tragedy into my heavenly treasure.

When Justin's book was to be released, an editor suggested I leave off the epilogue that told of the divorce, because it was just too sad to lose a child and then also lose a marriage. I agreed it was sad but it was also the truth. I couldn't ethically publish a book about God's goodness during Justin's lifetime and just fail to mention that my marriage didn't survive.

*Where storm clouds gather, rainbows abound.*

I have been glad many times that I didn't shortchange the truth. Every time I speak, someone in the audience says, "You just told my story, and I thought I was the only one." I later learned that the death of a child is so traumatic that eighty percent of all couples who lose a child separate within one year; most divorce—even in Christian homes.

Remember, though, that where storm clouds gather, rainbows abound. One of my rainbows as we gathered to mourn Justin's passing was knowing that my mother-in-law was in heaven. I know Jesus is there, and I know all our needs are supplied. I don't know if babies in heaven need baths, but I had seen my mother-in-law tenderly bathe a baby. Strange as it seems, that image brought me comfort in the midst of my pain. Someone I know and love was there, caring for my child. To my broken mother heart she was Jesus with skin on.

## How Do These Troubles Affect Our Children?

Initially children will cope by thinking that what happened to them is the way life is. They will think everyone's mother dies, everyone's brother goes to heaven. They may ask questions related to their limited understanding: "When will I die so I can go to heaven?" "Can I watch Jesus pick up the flowers we left at the cemetery?" "Why won't Jesus let him come back home?" These are questions of confusion, not questions of deep grief.

*One of the best things we can do to help our children is to get help for ourselves.*

As they cope with their loss, children may have times of tears or spurts of anger. They may periodically act out. Something may trigger their grief, such as a holiday, a place, a game that reminds them of the person who died, or even an aroma.

After they have worked through their grief, children will have become more in tune with their emotions. They will cry readily, in a healthy way. They will develop a lifestyle of owning their emotions, incorporating the new reality into their lives, and moving on. They will be guided by what they have learned; perhaps it will affect their choice of career. But they will remember . . . they will always remember.

If they do not work through their grief and cry their tears, children will live a life out of weakness rather than strength. They may be extremely passive or extremely aggressive, rigid or immoral, overly emotional or cold, depressed or hyperactive.

## What Should We Teach Our Children?

It is important, when the storms of life come, that we model healthy grief and healthy recovery for our children so they will have a role model. But this book is about helping children, not about us—or is it? One of the best things we can do to help our children is to get help for ourselves. We are their role models, and we want them to grow up whole. All of life is not happy. It is important that, mostly by example, we teach our children the many lessons of hope:

> The only real failure is falling down one more time than
>     you get up.
> God didn't cause this, but he will walk through it with you.
> God loves you very much. You will be happy again.
> It is smart to get help when your heart is broken.
> "Laughter is the best medicine." [Thanks, Art Linkletter!]
> "Some days are like that, even in Australia." [Thanks, Judith
>     Viorst!]

When hurricanes wrack the eastern seashore, the towns in the path board up. Residents plan to wait out the storm, then get on with the business of rebuilding. There are times in our lives when we need to do that. Wait out the storm. Cry our tears. Do whatever's next. Let people in to love and help us. Then when the storm subsides, begin to rebuild.

It is amazing that God's grace can forgive, cleanse, and heal. It is awesome that God can grow beauty from the ashes of our lives. It is comforting to know that he feels what we do.

I once commented to a dear friend that I didn't understand why God would cause all this to happen to me. She replied, "Oh, Sherry, God didn't cause this. I believe there were tears in heaven the day your marriage died."

Thinking of God with tears of sorrow for me helped me understand those days when he was silent. His heart too was broken over the choice of one of his children. He also knows that when we rage at him, demanding an explanation, what we really want is an argument. He refuses to yell back at us—but in hindsight we realize he carried us through.

---

*Troubles do seem to come in bundles. One of the children I work with is a perfect example of "bundles of troubles." He was placed in a residential treatment facility because his mom didn't know what else to do with him. Shortly after he came to this treatment center, his father, who was the only person he felt he got along with, was arrested and eventually served time for drug dealing. Larry had a lot of difficulties trying to fit in with the rest of the kids. His parents never told him they loved him or cared about him. He had no self-esteem whatsoever.*

*During the time he was with us, we tried many ways to reach him, including telling him we were proud of him, encouraging him, and letting him know that he deserved to be cared about. He was eventually able to return home to his mother, and as he left, he told us that the only reason he was able to survive was because the staff cared for him, always encouraged him, and were never afraid to tell him he was worth something. I know we made a difference in his life. I pray that because of our love he will one day be able to believe that God loves him.*

*When life's difficulties come, I still tend to shut down and not do nice things for myself. I have trouble seeing the big picture and knowing it won't last forever. I tend to shy away from those who are close to me, in order to avoid causing them unnecessary grief. When I finally reach out for help, things are huge, but they are always easier to face with those who love and believe in me.*

*When troubles come in bundles, make sure you let your children know that you love them, and just be there to hold them when the hurt sinks into their little hearts. Do the best you can to both let your children know and remind yourself that this too shall pass and there will be some wonderful, glorious days to come. Do not lose hope in what is to come through the sovereignty of Christ.*

## Chapter 4

# Life's Not Fair

*It was a time of joy. We were seeing a friend's new baby for the first time. His five-year-old brother was one of Jeff's buddies, so that made him extra special.*

*"Look, Jeff," I said. "Isn't Stevie's little brother cute!"*

*"Ya, Mom."*

*Jeff talked to him for a moment as I watched. We both made baby faces, enjoying the awesomeness and beauty of new life.*

*Soon a little tug came at my pant leg. In a concerned voice Jeff asked, "Mom, when will Stevie's brother go to heaven?"*

---

Aunt Margie and Uncle Alton are my mentors, friends, and adopted parents. I lived with my mother and my grandparents through high school graduation but spent many weekends with Margie and Alton. When I left for college, I lived with them during holidays. In fact, I still spend holidays with them; Jeff calls them Grandpa and Grandma. I've been so blessed; although abandoned by my father before I was even born, I had a good mother, godly grandparents, and wonderful adopted parents. I needed them all!

Alton says one reason he believes in heaven is because life is so unfair, there has to be a place where it all evens out. We adults know that, but in our small children it is expressed in questions or behaviors like Jeff's in the incident described above. Our response must embrace our curious children, own our personal pain, and teach them to love at the risk of losing. Not an easy task!

> *Our response must embrace our curious children, own our personal pain, and teach them to love at the risk of losing.*

I have been blessed with a host of very talented and wonderful nieces and nephews. They all came into the world with me cheering. Those born after Justin's death came into the world with an extra dose of cheering, praying, and thanking God for their safe arrival.

My nephew Scott was born prematurely and got a staph infection in the hospital. We didn't know for several weeks if he would live. I can still close my eyes and see him the day we brought him home. I remember spending hours rocking him and crying, partly because I was so grateful that he made it, partly because I was missing my own son who didn't.

## What About Sympathy?

Before my tragedy I felt sorry for those whose life circumstances brought them pain. After watching Justin demand his right to live against all odds, I realize that pity is an insult. I look at someone smiling from a wheelchair, someone reading with fingers, someone signing to communicate, and I beam with admiration. They appear to love so completely and unselfishly. Surely they give us the key to life as God intended it.

I watch a family with a broken heart reach a place where they don't hide from their pain, where they have learned to love at the risk of losing, where they can talk through their tears, and I empathize—but I don't pity. I admire! I salute their bravery. I know now how much courage it takes to bridge that chasm between our pain and our relationships.

When we hide from those who are hurting, we are pitying. We are afraid of our own emotions. We are living in fear.

Sympathy says, "I'm sorry." That's good.

Empathy says, "I cry with and for you. I trust you to grow through this tragedy." That's better.

When Justin was born and our time of sorrow intensified, my husband and I made a decision. Our friends were afraid to ask us to baby-sit, because they didn't want to remind us of our loss. We decided that we would do the asking. We periodically called them, asking if they needed a night out and volunteering to baby-sit. We needed a baby to love. We refused to allow ourselves to become the objects of pity and to become bitter because others had what we did not.

## What Should We Teach Our Children?

- It's okay, normal, healthy to cry about your loss.
- It is *not* okay to use it as an excuse for failure.
- Life's not fair. It hurts. I'm sorry. I wish you didn't have to feel the pain.
- You must move on, but I know you'll never forget.
- Use your sorrow for good, not for evil.
- We can be happy for Stevie and sad for us at the same time.

For the sake of ourselves and our children, we must reach out to Stevie's brother, mother, father, and Stevie to say, "Can we love you, too?"

How did I respond to Jeff's question about his friend's brother? The pain of Jeff's words cut me deeply. My response brought him into our decision to love at the risk of losing: "We hope Stevie's brother won't go to heaven for a very long time, don't we? I wouldn't like it if Stevie's family had to hurt the way we do when we miss our Justin."

In the words of Dr. Schuller, "Life's not fair, but God is good."[4]

---

*Those who are hurting seem to have a real insight into life, and I enjoy talking to them. I'm very understanding of the grief and pain that goes with life, and supportive of those around me when they are in need of help.*

*As I grew and more of life's grief happened to me, I learned that life's not fair. I know now that when unfair things occur, I need to get back to where I want to be instead of dwelling on the tragedy.*

*It is very important to validate the feelings of your children. Your children will be blunt and truthful with how they feel. If they tell you they hate God for taking their sibling, then that's exactly how they feel. Don't punish them for saying such things, because you also at some point will be just as angry and frustrated with God, placing the blame on him. Allowing your children to deal honestly with their very confusing and frustrating feelings will make them much more sensitive and concerned adults, able to carry on their lives in productive and healthy ways.*

## Chapter 5

# Grief Comes in Waves

*Three years ago my niece gave birth to Breanne, our first family grandchild. Jeff commented to me, "You know, Mom, one of the things that makes me sad is that I'll never be an uncle."*

---

The waves of grief don't come as often after time separates us from our heartache, but they do come. They come with every celebration ("Dad won't be here to walk me down the aisle") and with every birth ("I'll never be an uncle"). With every new sorrow, old hurt is rekindled ("I had a sister who died, too; I was ten").

Hollywood periodically deals with these issues. The movie *Stepparent* has a particularly poignant scene. Julia Roberts, the step-parent, and Susan Sarandon, the mother dying of cancer, make peace with one another. Julia says, "I have this fear that I'll be standing over her fixing her wedding veil one day, telling her she's the most beautiful bride in the world. And all the time she'll be wishing I was you." Susan's response: "My fear is that she won't."

Hopefully, she will deeply love them both and cherish a wonderful stepmother. But she will never get over missing her mom.

Time and grief work transform the event from unbearable sorrow to a memory, but love never dies. It is wonderful that you have a good stepmother who loves you, but it is sad that your mother died. The two coexist; one does not negate the other.

> *Time and grief work transform the event from unbearable sorrow to a memory, but love never dies.*

Grief creeps up on you. One minute you are fine, enjoying the adventure of life. The next moment tears of grief spill down your face. I spent so many years trying to stifle my tears, wondering why grief didn't go away and why I wasn't strong enough to control it. Now I just give myself permission to cry.

I spent many hours trying to make Jeff's days so wonderful and fun-filled that he wouldn't have time to miss his brother. Now I give him permission to wonder what might have been.

## How Is Grief Expressed in Children?

With every new stage in life, these waves of grief come bearing a new face. They are triggered at every major life transition: when our children achieve a landmark accomplishment (blue ribbon, recital, graduation, etc.); when they move to a new stage in their relationships (first date, engagement, wedding, parenthood, etc.); and when they undergo physical changes (puberty, growing into adulthood, childbearing, etc.).

In young children grief sometimes comes out in misbehavior. They pick fights, walk out of a store with something in their pocket, or sit in class staring off into space. We must deal with the behaviors to teach important lessons about life, but we should also begin asking some grief questions:

What did he say that made you want to punch him?

What were you thinking when you walked out of the store without paying?

What were you daydreaming about while you sat in class doing nothing?

Sometimes they don't know, so we need to ask them feeling questions. Begin thinking about what might have triggered it:

Are you missing Daddy?

Are you sad because the story reminded you of Grandpa? We've been talking about how it would have been his sixty-fifth birthday.

Are you angry with Sam, or are you really angry with Justin for not being here?

## How Long Do the Waves of Grief Keep Coming?

Memories are forever! Jeff was twenty-three in the little story that began this chapter. Now, though, he can own his grief, talk about it, and cry if he needs to; he doesn't need to pick fights because his heart is hurting.

And Breanne considers him one of her favorite uncles! You can never have too many big people spoil you. Who knows when Mom and Dad will say no and you'll need an extra uncle to get your way?

———

*My whole life, I have known that I would never be a real uncle. In my earlier years this caused some anger because I had to deal with the ever-so-hard-to-answer question of why.*

*Arguing with God over that question really hasn't helped me come up with any clear answers, other than this: There are people in my family who by blood* are cousins but whom I refer to as aunts and uncles. I don't know them as anything else. They are the real thing. Over the years God has helped me come to peace with the fact that one day I too would be a cousin who is called Uncle Jeff, and to those who call me Uncle Jeff, I too would be the real thing. Knowing that has brought me so much peace in my soul.

The waves of grief do creep up on you. Always I remember on Justin's birthday. Sometimes on Christmas, out of the blue, I'll think of him and begin to cry. Sometimes I don't know what triggers it. I just know that although he is dead, he is very alive. I want to live my life so I'll see him again. I want him to be proud of his big bro!

In the tough time of death, it is important for the children you care about to constantly be surrounded by people who will care for them and help them build healthy relationships. Without this kind of support it will be much more difficult for them to fully understand and come to terms with death.

## Chapter 6

# Good-bye Is Not Forever!

*God* hath not promised skies always blue, but he hath promised strength for today."

My mind was fuzzy but I recognized my grandmother's voice. I struggled to open my eyes or call out to her.

"Just remember, 'All things work together for good.'"

That was Margie, my adopted mom. Again I struggled but against a body that would not work.

I heard Pappy, my father-in-law, say, "My mommie always told me . . ."; then the voice changed and Grandmommie, his mother, said, "Sonny, his grace is sufficient."

I struggled for consciousness and finally managed to open my eyes.

As I began to awaken from the anesthetic, I could hear nurses talking, but try as I might, words refused to find my mouth. I could feel my body spasm but could do nothing to control it. Finally I found I could move my head, and I looked around the room trying to find Gram . . . or Margie . . . or Pappy. I had just heard them speak to me, and their voices rang with assurance, but they weren't there.

And then I began to remember. I struggled as thoughts and words raced through my mind, but I couldn't find a way to get them out of my mouth. When words finally came, I winced at their reality. A strange, faint voice from inside me asked, "Is my baby alive?"

*And I cringed in fear of either answer.*

*The nurses responded quickly, kindly, and precisely. They told me the baby had been born alive and was a boy. Then they abandoned me to my thoughts and fears as one of them rushed to summon the doctor. I sensed fear in them, too; they were as afraid of my questions as I was of their answers.*

*They acted almost mechanical around me; their words rang in my ears as I lay alone. A strange numbness had control of my body. I could hear; uncensored thoughts and questions raced through my mind. But speaking, feeling, reacting, or moving were foreign to me.*

*Recent memories hammered at my consciousness now, reminding me where I was and why I was here. Earlier, in the delivery room, I was shocked to hear the words "I fear your baby is hydrocephalic. If it's born alive, it probably won't live long."*

*As those words stabbed at my heart, a strange and beautiful peace surrounded me. I became aware of God's holy presence filling the room. Something from deep inside me whispered, "You'll make it." I begged it to shout, "The doctors are wrong! You'll awaken to find the baby happy and healthy; this is just a bad nightmare." Denial is the first stage of grief.*

*The Holy Presence, however, did not take the fact of my loss away. Rather, in my moment of need God gave me the assurance that he was able to handle the situation and was in control. He gave me the knowledge that he had the power to bring me through. He surrounded me with the peace that passes understanding (Philippians 4:7).*

---

Yes, this is a true story. This is about me, not about Jeff. This was in the recovery room after Justin was born. The voices were real and audible. Grandmommie had been dead for five years.

In a recent work-related class, my coworkers and I participated in an exercise in values. We were instructed to write the twelve most important things in our lives on slips of paper and spread them out in front of us. Then we were asked, "If you had to give up one, which one would it be?" This question was repeated again and again. We would, one piece of paper at a time and laboriously, take away the least impor-tant thing. With each round, the class didn't proceed until everyone had removed some-thing, so those of us who hesitated held up the progress of the entire group. In the final round the instructor pressured us to remove everything.

*I had never before thought of heaven's treasures in terms of people. Now I can't imagine anything more valuable.*

I found I could easily give up my things. When it came to people, it was a deep strug-gle. I finally realized that although it was painful, I could give up the people in my life. The last person I let go of was Jeff. Rationally I couldn't do it. But I'd had no choice when I let go of Justin. Because of his death and my recovery, I realized I could let go of a loved one so long as I never let go of my faith.

The instructor kept prodding. "Give up your faith. I want you to see what it's like to be hopeless."

I responded, "I know what hopeless is, and I never need to go there again. Through my hopelessness I deepened my faith. I'm a Christian. I believe we'll meet again. I can let go of the people I love on earth because I know I'm not *really* letting them go. We'll meet again. We'll be together in eternity!"

## What Does It Mean to Have Treasures in Heaven?

At Justin's memorial the pastor spoke of us now having a lit-tle treasure in heaven that we would someday be able to claim. I had never before thought of heaven's treasures in terms of people. Now I can't imagine anything more valuable.

I have a little treasure who is being raised in heaven. God has graciously granted me the privilege of raising another treasure on earth. My job as a parent is to sow seeds of hope in Jeff's heart so that when he too goes through tough times, he will remember my teachings and gain strength from my faith.

Today heaven is a near and dear place to me. I have a little treasure there. Someday when it's my turn to go, I'll hear that treasure call, "Mom!"

Billy Graham says, in his book *Angels,* that those we have loved on earth accompany the angels as they usher us into another kingdom.[5]

Peter Marshall says, "Those we love are with the Lord, and the Lord has promised to be with us. If they are with Him, and He is with us, they are never really very far away."

## How Does God Plant Eternity in the Hearts of Our Children?

The time came when, sitting in another hospital room, I recognized that again a strange and beautiful sense of peace had filled me and that God's holy presence filled the room. I was holding my baby boy just before he was to have his fifth major surgery. Children's Hospital in Fresno, California, had become our second home. I finally could give of my love without reservation, and even though I tried to deny it, the Holy Presence whispered that I was holding my son for the last time on earth. I sat in the midst of the peace that passes understanding—loving my baby, soaking in his love, enjoying his being, and basking in God's presence, in an hour of solitude.

This time I had no thoughts of running. This time I had no intention to forget. This time I wanted to love forever and would accept each day as it came. This time I didn't hear the voices, but I drew strength from their memory as I thanked God for my heritage and told my son what I thought heaven would be like. This time I claimed him as my precious, priceless son and did all I could to convey that wordless love that flows between mother and child. And yes, this time too I felt so helpless and wished with all my heart that I could give my life to make his easier.

When I invested myself wholeheartedly in the child I had given to God, something divine happened. The love of God flowed through that tiny, helpless, deformed life and filled my soul.

The ordeal has ended; the mourning is passed. The memory and love remain. In working through my grief, I have often thought of this experience in prayer. I have wished so many times that God would talk audibly with me, but he speaks in mysterious ways, and often we fail to recognize his voice.

Once in prayer I remembered those voices and asked, "Lord, why wasn't it your voice I heard?"

I was reminded of a passage in Deuteronomy 11 that commands God's people to teach his word to their children. My family had done that.

*I had heard the voice of God spoken, so sweetly, through those whose faith I had learned to trust as a child.*

Simply, quietly, the truth dawned. I had heard the voice of God spoken, so sweetly, through those whose faith I had learned to trust as a child. I am deeply and eternally blessed.

Ecclesiastes 3:11 says, "He has made everything beautiful in its time. He has also set eternity in the hearts of men." Eternity is planted one word, one hug, one laugh, one tear at a time. When we are blessed with godly parents, God does it through them.

*No dreams will e'er be shattered by dark or dreary days.*
*The light will vanish all the doubt.*
*Just travel up the road 'til you reach the land of gold.*
*There you'll see the God behind the clouds.*

"CLOUDS" BY THE CHOIR, FROM THE CD *CHASE THE KANGAROO*[6]

*God gave my mother quite a sense of peace in that recovery room. The light of God somehow vanished all her fear and doubt. He helped her realize that once she reaches the land of gold, she will get to see the God behind the clouds. And she will hear my little brother calling out, "Mom!" That will bring us one step closer to what my great-grandfather prayed for daily: reuniting the family circle in heaven. I believe that the reunion of my mother, brother, and me will be cheered by all who have seen the grief and strife we have gone through.*

*Music is powerful to me. There are some songs that remind me in a very strong and vivid way of times in my life, both good and bad. I tend to relive the feelings I had or the events I experienced when I first heard these songs. Music gives me strength. It plays a huge part in how I cope with tough times. In order for me to survive the bad times, I surround myself with caring friends and family and try hard to listen to the music that I associate with the good and happy times of my life.*

*I think it is important to encourage children to listen to music. It somehow penetrates a person's soul. I have been around music my whole life and am grateful. After my grandmother's funeral, when I listened to a song that the two of us always enjoyed together, it somehow made the sadness of her death a little easier to bear. I was thirteen; the song helped me remember the good and fun times we had together. I think music is an important part of every child's life. Parents should listen to their children's music, even if they don't like or understand it. My mom and I traded music days in the car, but we each had veto power if a song came on that we really couldn't stand. You never know when one of those crazy songs your kids listen to will be the comfort they need when they are dealing with a death.*

*Part 2*

## Tough Questions Parents Ask

*W̃e were in the hospital coping with the tragic news that Justin was hydro-cephalic and probably wouldn't live. We agonized over every decision. Should we—could we—bring him home and watch him die? Institutionalize him? Place him in a home for handicapped children where we could visit? We wondered what was right; every choice seemed so wrong. We knew we had to make some decision, but what?*

*One night I expressed to a friend my concern about doing God's will. By the time we finished our conversation, I had an entirely new understanding of Scripture. She shared the verses leading up to Romans 8:28—verses I had read many times but never really heard:*

> In the same way, the Spirit helps us in our weakness. We do not know what we ought to pray for, but the Spirit himself intercedes for us with groans that words cannot express. And he who searches our hearts knows the mind of the Spirit, because the Spirit intercedes for the saints in accordance with God's will.
>
> ROMANS 8:26–27

*She explained that when we are in Christ, we can make any decision—even a selfish one. Then if we truly give it to him, he will reverse it if we err, will intercede with God according to what we meant rather than what we said, and will work it out for good.*

*As we prayed to discern what would be the "right decision," we learned that the Holy Spirit understands all languages—even the language of tears.*

---

In the midst of the whirlwind of decisions that confront us during grief, we parents find ourselves modeling for our children those lessons we learned in our homes of origin. Sometimes we had wonderful role models. Sometimes, however, our early teaching was not wise. In some cases it was harmful. As we enter the world of grief, we must search for answers so we can provide our children with healthy coping patterns. What we do, our children will do—and so will our grandchildren. For their sake we must make it through victoriously.

> *The Holy Spirit understands all languages— even the language of tears.*

Making the decision of what to do with Justin was gut-wrenching. We decided to place him in a home for handicapped children. I didn't want to do that, but I was so fearful about caring for him. This seemed to be a good alternative. The sweet lady who took care of him taught me how to watch for health signs, instilled me with hope, and made it possible for Justin to come home for two and a half months. God did more than reverse our initial decision. He used it to train me. I really wanted Justin to come home, but I didn't know how to communicate with the doctors, care for a critically ill child, and ask for help. Mrs. Sperling taught me how. She was an oasis in the process of God's working out our choice for good.

The decisions relating to Jeff after Justin died, although not as traumatic, were harder. They were harder because there weren't right answers. They were harder because I sometimes reacted emotionally. When I did, he learned not to talk. When I would ask him why he hadn't talked with me, he would say, "Mom, it kills your gut!" It did, but we still needed to face it together.

This section, "Tough Questions Parents Ask," is born of that learning.

---

*The children I work with have never learned how to deal with their emotions; they don't have a healthy understanding of how to process them. They only understand violence as a way to deal with feelings they don't totally comprehend. They think that every time they get angry, they have to get into a physical confrontation, rather than taking the time to figure out what's bothering them. I am in a role in which I can help them learn what their trigger points are and that it is okay to be mad but the way they channel that anger will decide whether they get into trouble or not.*

*Had many of these children had the example of appropriate and healthy ways to deal with anger and emotions, chances are they would not be in residential treatment today. They would be leading productive and healthy lives rather than being a destructive part of their environment. It is very important that parents allow their children to feel, and teach them how to deal with these feelings. If children wait until they are grown, they must change a lifestyle of destructive patterns.*

## Chapter 7

# What About Tears—
# Theirs and Ours?

*J*eff and I joined my adopted sister Karen on a much-needed mini vacation in Palm Springs. Life was settling down to what would become our new normal, but grief was still too fresh for me to feel comfortable leaving Jeff with a baby-sitter while we enjoyed the evening entertainment. Ordering tickets to see a college production of West Side Story, I reasoned, "He'll be asleep before the first scene is over."

*Wrong!* He was enthralled with live theater. During intermission he chatted nonstop about one of the principal characters, Tony:

"Mom, have you met my new friend Tony?"

"Mom, can Tony come to our house?"

*I was enchanted by my adorable elfin child. He was so cute living this new experience that I forgot my own grief for a while.*

*Then intermission ended. As I walked him down the aisle to our seats, it suddenly hit me: Tony will die.*

*The entire last half of the play, I whispered nonstop in Jeff's ear:*

*"Jeff, you know this is pretend, don't you?"*

*"Jeff, you know this isn't real, don't you?"*

*"Jeff, this isn't really happening; it's just a play."*

*"Jeff . . ."*

*Nevertheless, the last scene arrived. The ruckus occurred; the gun sounded; Tony died onstage.*

*Jeff shrieked, burst into tears, and sobbed in agony.*

*The audience erupted in laughter.*

*Tony was neither happy nor understanding that a traumatized child had transformed his dying scene from tragedy to comedy. He wasn't even nice when I took Jeff backstage to see that he was indeed still alive.*

---

It is so difficult to empathize and allow tears to flow; to sit silently while grief is expressed; to listen to another's irrational ramblings. If we do that, we must share in another person's pain.

## Why Are We Afraid to Express Our Grief?

- We are afraid we will lose control.
- We are afraid of looking foolish in front of others.
- We have been taught to tough it out and that big boys don't cry. In fact, we have been taught a lot of things that are outright lies.
- We have been taught that we laugh in public and cry in the privacy of our own rooms.
- We live in a world that intellectualizes. We are more comfortable exposing our heads than our hearts.

However, if we bury our grief, it lives quietly within us until something in life triggers it. During those trigger times we either face it or run from it. Grief will find its release. Those who run from their emotional pain bear it as illnesses or personality disorders for the rest of their lives.

Let's help our children express their emotions, questions, feelings, memories, fears. That way, tears and the related loss become a part of their life rather than a veil that separates them from living a happy and meaningful life.

## What Is the Typical Grief Process?

Current researchers focus on the differences in grief and on the reality that each person has the right to grieve in his or her own way. However, although it's true that no two people grieve alike, there are commonalities in all grief. Dr. Elisabeth Kübler-Ross—who, through research on patients who were terminally ill, first identified what we now call the grief cycle—focused on these commonalities. In later years many scientists, psychologists, and doctors have repeated her research in other situations, confirming that there is a universal, similar process that all adults go through to cope with change in their lives.

Although in words it sounds like a neat little cycle, in reality this process is a spiral repeated many times in varying degrees and different intensities over a period of years. Typically, adults who are dying and adults who watch a loved one die go through six broad stages: shock and denial, emotional reactions, bargaining, depression, acceptance, and recovery.

### Shock and Denial

The stage of shock and denial gives people superhuman energy to get through their crisis, the ability to speak and greet guests at the funeral, and a general feeling of well-being that masks the intensity of emotions. It is God's gift to us in our time of need. In the Bible we observe the denial process in the disciples after Jesus' crucifixion. They went back to fishing; it was the only life they knew without him. In our stage of shock, we go back to who we were before our loved one was a part of our life and work through our grief to the present time.

### Emotional Reactions

Once reality sets in, the stage of emotional reactions can be observed. We may be angry with our loved one for dying; we may be relieved that they don't have to suffer anymore. We may feel both at the same time. Often we are relieved that we don't have to go to the hospital every day—which of course feeds our feelings of guilt. We would go to the hospital every day of our lives if only we could have back the one we love. Any emotion, good or bad, is normal. It's also normal to feel nothing—that simply means we're still in the stage of denial. Emotions aren't right or wrong. They just are. It is how we express them that can be healthy or hurtful.

One of my favorite passages in the Bible is John 11:35: "Jesus wept." It doesn't matter what translation we read; it says the same thing. I could preach a sermon on that one passage, and I'm not even a preacher! We don't need to feel guilty for having emotions. God gave them to us, and Jesus wept.

### Bargaining

As long as there is hope, we live in the bargaining stage. We beg God to spare the life of our loved one. We promise God we will make changes in our lives, we'll tithe or go to church every Sunday or support an orphan, if . . . Sometimes when we bargain God says yes, sometimes wait, sometimes no. In I Samuel 1:11 Hannah bargained with God for a son. God graciously granted her request and gave her Samuel. In Matthew 26:39 Jesus bargained with God to spare him the agony of the cross. God said no. Aren't you glad he did!

### Depression

When our efforts at bargaining don't work and our loved one dies, we enter the stage of depression. We may feel abandoned by God because he didn't answer our prayers. We may be angry with ourselves for not having been able to get medical help in time or for an act of neglect. We may just be tired because we have been under so much stress for such a long time and we need to rest. Reactive depression feels like a little black cloud is following us around. We worry about ourselves. Reactive depression is actually a gift we've earned; it's the body's way of regrouping. It will lift as quickly as it came once our grief work is completed. If we are depressed for more than a year, we may need medical attention. Elijah, in I Kings 19, fled to Horeb and begged God to let him die. God didn't scold him for his exhaustion-based depression. Rather God told him to eat, sleep, and wait on his still, small voice.

### Acceptance

When we work through the stages of our grief, we reach acceptance. It is sad that this happened, but it is also true. We will learn from it; we will grow. We will move on, but we will never forget. Jesus' words of acceptance were, "My Father, if it is not possible for this cup to be taken away unless I drink it, may your will be done" (Matthew 26:42).

### Recovery

Recovery is the process of learning and growing from our experience and moving on with life. In the words of King David, "While the child was still alive, I fasted and wept. I thought, 'Who knows? The LORD may be gracious to me and let the child live.' But now that he is dead, why should I fast? Can I bring him back again? I will go to him, but he will not return to me" (2 Samuel 12:22–23).

## What Are Age-Typical Responses to Grief?

Just as there are commonalities in the grief of all adults, underneath the masks of childhood there are common characteristics of grief that are based on a child's emotional age at the time of the loss. Understanding these will enable us to help our children through their grief.

### The Age of Helplessness

Babies and toddlers, helpless to care for their own needs, learn that they will be cared for in response to their cries. This is an important lesson in trust, building the foundation for positive responses to an adult world. The death of a caretaker produces great fear in children between the ages of one and two, especially in boys. In addition to feeling the loss, they feel unprotected. They need consistency and continuity in their lives. These children will have to revisit their grief during adolescence.

Make sure adults who love a bereaved infant spend a lot of time holding, hugging, and admiring him or her. An infant's sense of worth is developed from adult admiration.

### The Age of Guilt

Between the ages of three and five, children learn the difference between good and bad. With this knowledge comes guilt. As their sexual identities evolve, these children often fall in love with the parent of the opposite sex. Thus little boys may fantasize that their father will disappear, leaving them free to marry their mother. Little girls in turn fantasize that they will marry their father. If the parent of the opposite sex does indeed die, these children feel as though they caused it. If they were jealous of a sibling who dies, they may believe they killed him or her. They commonly experience nightmares, a reflection of their guilt-laced fears. Children in this age group have a tendency to express their emotional needs by randomly reaching out to new adults, climbing into the laps of strangers, and expressing a need for physical contact, nurturing, and protection.

Jeff was three when his brother died. When I tried to talk to him about it, he would talk about something else. I thought he didn't understand, thus didn't feel the hurt. As I observed him playing with another adult, it became obvious that he was intentionally changing the subject every time an emotional issue emerged.

Encourage your children to verbalize their fears and feelings as a natural part of play. They may tell a doll what troubles them or express their confusion to an adult while swinging, building a fort, or reading a bedtime story. Their drawings may be filled with their fears and guilt. This is healthy because children are expressing rather than repressing their grief. Children at this age are also old enough to deny their feelings, especially if they have observed a pattern of denial in one of their parents. Since children of this age identify with right and wrong, this is a good time to introduce them to Jesus. Encourage them to talk to God about things that trouble them. We don't have answers or power to change thinking; he does.

### The Age of Sadness

Children between the ages of six and eight express great sadness when someone dies. Normally this is a quiet time in their development. They have successfully completed kindergarten, their first step in gaining independence, and are in a restful stage before the onset of puberty. Their primary developmental tasks are to move toward independence from their family and to firm up their self-concepts. They rely on a strong home structure for protection and comfort after school. If that home structure is threatened, they are left feeling helpless, angry, fearful, and betrayed. But above all, bereaved children at this age feel sad. They are too old to escape through fantasy; they are not yet old enough to go through an adult grieving process. Instead they tend to retreat into depression. If the parents of a child of this age hide personal feelings of loss, the child will learn similar patterns of masking emotion—patterns that will have a long-range consequence. If, on the other hand, a parent's grief is inconsolable, the child feels insecure. Children at this age have difficulty expressing anger toward their caretakers, but they often express extreme anger to friends and extended family and sometimes even to pets.

In the delightful book *Dear God*, Cindy, age eight, writes,

Dear God,
My Grandma died a year ago. My mom says she is with you. Could you give her this letter?
Here is the letter:

Grandma,
I'm doing good in school and I met a boy I'm going to marry. All my love.[7]

Engage these children in age-appropriate play activities, listen a lot, and help them with schoolwork. These children will be eager learners of social skills. They will enjoy hearing touching or funny stories, especially about the deceased. Teach them to tell a good joke. Life in a bereaved home is often void of laughter, and a home without laughter is sad.

### The Age of Anger
Between the ages of nine and twelve, children are finally able to see that death is not their fault. Abandoned, the child reacts, understandably, in anger. At this age children are usually quite

verbal about their hostility over a death and are able to talk to a third party, even though they may try to hide their feelings from their parents. Their expression of anger may take the form of extreme activity. But in spite of their busyness, they suffer feelings of shame, resentment, rejection, loneliness, and even exhaustion. They may be pushed into an adult role that they are not yet ready to handle.

Sometimes in children sorrow is expressed as anger. It embarrasses him today, but my eight-year-old nephew, in response to my question, "Do you miss Grandma?" responded, "Nope! I hate her!" I hugged him rather than scolded him. I knew it was his language of tears. We need to teach our children how to cry, or those tears will go inside and destroy them.

Teach these children appropriate ways to express their anger. Talking about it, writing letters—especially Dear God letters—are good ways to express anger. Make sure that when they physically express anger (such as by hitting golf balls, hammering nails, doing yard work, etc.), they also verbalize it. Physical expression helps deal with the pent-up energy, but until they verbalize anger, the pain is still there. In short, anything that works for adults can work for children as well, but they need guidance.

### The Age of False Maturity

Psychologists term the teen years as the age of false maturity. Adolescence is often a difficult time when family life is stable. A death in the family during the period of adolescence may intensify the turbulence and stress for both generations. It may postpone the child's maturing and detaching from parents, or it may speed up the process. At this age children usually experience some form of the traditional grief cycle. Teens who were emotionally healthy before a death and do not bury their initial grief will not usually suffer permanent personality damage, even though they will suffer a great loss. However, when teenagers react to loss in their lives, they may get into very adult problems. There is a possibility that they will become involved in self-abusive behaviors such as premature sexual activity, drinking, or drugs.

When nineteen-year-old Staci's grandma died, Staci appeared to deal normally with her grief. Then one month later she opened credit cards in every major store in the mall and charged them to the limit. She became belligerent and slept a lot. These are symptoms of grief turned inward. Thankfully, her family recognized this as a grief reaction and is encouraging her to get counseling and take responsibility for her debt.

Friends can help by keeping teenagers busy—very busy. An active church program is vital. In addition, teens benefit from a support group in which they can share their frustration with other teens and loving adults. Teenagers need to be taught adult responses to loss, especially how to express their anger and how to deal with guilt. Above all, they need to be encouraged to share their feelings, good and bad, with the Lord and with one or two trusted friends.

Don't assume children are fine because you don't see signs of trouble. Although it is true that time heals once an issue is confronted, grief festers if it is denied rather than expressed; it does not go away. The child whose initial reaction appears too good to be true may be headed for serious trouble later in life.

## What About Our Tears?

Children are quick to mimic our behavior. I broke a few annoying habits shortly after I became a mother. It's strange how quickly I was motivated when I walked in my shadow! A child will deal with death, too, using our example. If we are brave in front of them and don't let them see us cry, we teach them to bury their emotions rather than express them. If we go to the other extreme and grieve uncontrollably, we shut them out of our lives and lessen their self-worth. If we teach them that it's okay for girls and mommies to cry but boys and daddies have to be strong and comforting, we force them into behavior that has serious long-range consequences. Our daughters could use tears to manipulate and get their own way. Our boys could become macho caretakers.

*We decided it would be good for Jeff to know that Justin was in heaven and was now well. What we forgot to tell him was that we were not in heaven and that we would miss our baby for the rest of our lives.*

We decided it would be good for Jeff to know that Justin was in heaven and was now well. What we forgot to tell him was that *we* were not in heaven and that we would miss our baby for the rest of our lives. It would be okay if he did, too—so long as he did not let it destroy his ability to enjoy life now.

Each child has a special, unique way to deal with this thing called life. Regardless of circumstances or personality, however, the death of someone a child has loved cannot go unnoticed. Just as we had spent nine months preparing Jeff for his brother's birth, we would have to spend months—maybe years—helping him cope with his brother's death. Just as we must each grieve in our own way, so must a child grieve. A child will model what we do. If, in front of a child, we pretend it doesn't hurt, the child will respond by pretending it doesn't hurt. If he sees us coping with illness, pills, and alcohol, so he will cope, when he can, with illness, pills, and alcohol. We need to accept the fact that life must go on, and in the process of life's continuation it is okay to grieve and show our emotions so we may emerge stronger and more capable to enjoy today.

One of the most difficult lessons we must learn in life is that it is often unfair.

One of the greatest hopes we have in life is that God has glorious power to make us better and stronger in the midst of life's inequities.

One of the greatest hopes we have as parents is that God will use our example to bring hope and healing to our children. Whatever else you do, express your grief honestly. Pray that your children will learn that lesson earlier in life than you did.

---

*I remember going to see* West Side Story *and bursting into tears, thinking that this lead character, with whom for some reason I had bonded, died. I remember leaving the theater thinking that he was dead. I remember feeling a great sense of relief after I was brought backstage to find that indeed he was still alive. I am grateful to my mother for taking me backstage to see him.*

*Sadness is a strange thing. Sometimes I think we misunderstand what children are saying and brush it off as "Oh, he's so young, how can he know what sadness really is?" Children do know what sadness is and how it feels. The only thing that young age brings to a child is the lack of ability to explain what he or she feels. As children, we just know we feel sad and don't know what to do with it. That is why it's so important for parents to allow themselves to feel and express pain in front of their children.*

*One memory I have that will last forever is when a relative of mine had just lost a child. I must have been eight or nine at the time. We were at the graveside service for this baby. As everyone walked by to express their sorrow to the family, I was crying. The baby's dad was crying. He saw me as I walked by, and reached out and hugged me and held me in his lap as the two of us cried together, in public, showing me that it was okay to cry and be sad over things like a baby's death.*

———————

I remember that service, too. I was sad for the parents; I was sad for me; I was sad for Jeff. I remember him falling into Steve's arms and sobbing uncontrollably. It lasted for so long that I didn't know what to do. When I could finally pry him away so others could express their sorrow, Jeff's Grandpa Alton found us both, walked us a little ways away from the crowd, and held us and hugged us. I remember saying something about feeling sorry for Debi; Alton said, "I'm sorry for you too." In short, he gave us permission to express our own grief without shame.

Grief never really ends. With each new loss old grief is triggered. The only thing worse than going to another's funeral and crying would be not to go because you're afraid of tears.

## Chapter 8

# To Talk or Not to Talk?

*We were facing Justin's first birthday, and I was seeing a grief counselor. He asked how I would spend the day. I told him I would close my eyes and pray it would end quickly. He kindly reminded me that the day would happen, whether or not I faced it. Then he moved me to action: "If you could forget Justin, you could forget Jeff. You owe it to Jeff to face the day and celebrate the fact that Justin was born."*

*At his suggestion we baked Justin a birthday cake, sang "Happy Birthday," and talked about Justin; Jeff, his big brother, blew out his candle. I gave Jeff a little gift in honor of Justin.*

*But it wasn't happy. We were broken and lonely. Facing the day was right. Facing it with a birthday party, pretending we were happy when we were in deep pain, was wrong.*

---

The expression of grief is a difficult thing. We wear our bandages proudly when we have a broken arm or leg, but we are uncomfortable with our emotional pain and have trouble sharing our tears. We even tend to shush our children, thinking that if we help them forget, they won't hurt. Sometimes we shush them because we are embarrassed to talk in front of others. But shushing sends the tears inside, and the only thing worse than hurting alone is the deep soul loneliness when you hurt and think no one else cares or remembers.

## Why Is Communication Difficult?

When our children talk, they do three things that frustrate us.

1. They talk as though the person were still here, so we have to tell them again that the one we love is dead.
2. They chatter about things that are emotional to us, so we have to feel our own pain.
3. They ask us questions that surface our haunting fears, causing us to question if what we have always believed is really true.

These are our problems, not theirs. We need to keep this in mind so we can allow our children to talk out their curiosity. If they can do that, they will be better able to cry their tears. They will quickly assimilate death as a fact of life.

## Why Is Communication Necessary?

It is unnatural for a child not to talk about things; it just comes out! Mirth shares a memory of her grandfather dying when she was eight years old. Visiting him in the hospital, she knew instinctively that she wasn't supposed to say anything. But the moment she saw him, she started to cry and said, "Oh, Big Daddy, I don't want you to die!" Interestingly, most people who are dying want to talk about it, and most people who love someone who is dying can't. Probably Mirth's reaction was a great comfort to her grandfather.

I remember an incident when Jeff and I were driving to the cemetery where Justin was buried. We didn't go often, first because I couldn't handle it, then because we moved so far away. One day when Jeff was about eight, we had picked up balloons and were on our way to visit Justin's grave. As we drove, Jeff began to chatter nonstop.

"We're going to visit my brother Justin's grave. He died. We are very sad that he died. He was a good brother. He is buried in the ground. It makes us sad that he died...." Suddenly he stopped. He looked at me and said vehemently, "You're not going to cry again, are you, Mom?"

Children are constantly processing information at both a conscious and subconscious level. Sandra, at age nine, lost one of her close friends to bone cancer. She had phantom pains for several months. Her parents sent her to their church camp for one week the following summer. Since new experiences (like camp and being away from home) trigger grief, hers reappeared. Midweek her parents got a call to pick her up because she thought she had cancer, too. It is common for a child to fear he or she also will die following the death of one they love. As children develop into healthy adults, their grief will revisit them at every new stage in life. If it is not resolved through ongoing communication, reassurances, and lots of hugs, it could prohibit them from forming intimate friendships.

*The only thing worse than hurting alone is the deep soul loneliness when you hurt and think no one else cares or remembers.*

Betsy, as a young mother of two toddlers, watched a plane go down. Later that day she discovered it had carried her husband to his death. Her own grief was so raw; she was so young. She did the only thing she knew to do. She packed her memories, including pictures and documents, in a box and started over. When she moved, the box, still unopened, moved with her. She never shared it with her children. She didn't know she was supposed to. She didn't know how. Although she endeavored to help her children know about their father, she was afraid that if she shared too much, the dam inside her would burst and she would never quit crying.

She eventually remarried, had another child, and raised three beautiful and successful children. Her daughter became a financial planner. Part of her benefit package included free counseling, which she was undergoing. Betsy spoke to her about it, thinking she was dealing with the stress of the job. She wasn't. She was dealing with the death of her father.

Betsy resurrected the box and gave her children their heritage.

It's never too late to help your children. Grief will always be a part of their lives, but grief will lose its death hold on them once it is faced and mourned.

## How Do We Help Our Children to Talk?

In education we discuss the teachable moment. Look for those times when life hands you an opportunity to bring the subject up.

When a television show or movie brings tears of remembrance to your eyes, it is a good time to share with your children.

When children ask related questions, mention the one who died.

When they remind you of the good things about the deceased, tell them: "That mischievous grin of yours is just like Grandpa's."

When they express related fears, listen to the meaning behind them: "Mom, I have a headache" might mean simply that. It might mean, "I think I have a brain tumor, too."

Even arguments can lead to teachable moments. When children disagree with us but can't put their frustrations into words, they can sometimes sing it, draw it, write it, or act it out.

Friends report that their children talk more readily after a good back rub, while riding in a car, sitting at a soda fountain, walking together, or when they don't want to go to bed yet.

When children seem distressed but can't talk, a game may help them relax. The Ungame, a board game to help families communicate, is a great way to listen to your children's thoughts about life. Why is this particular game so great? Because you can't talk back until it's your turn and you draw a free card. You are forced just to listen. You learn a lot that way.

––––––––––

*A child I work with returned from his grandfather's funeral service. His grandpa was the one person that he felt had never stopped believing in him. The two of them had a special trip planned, but it came to a sudden end. Over the next several months this boy seemed to be okay, but when he mentioned his grandfather, he acted as if his grandpa had died a long time ago and he shouldn't be bothered by it anymore.*

*One night he had been missing his grandfather quite a bit. He really didn't want to talk about it, but I managed to help him open up, and we had an insightful talk. As he left our center to return home, I walked him out. He said, "Thanks for being there for me in the middle of my mess. Thanks for listening to me talk about my grandpa, too."*

*I remember as a child on several occasions needing to talk about being sad that Justin had died but deciding not to because I was afraid people would think I wasn't being serious about missing him. I think the most important thing you can do is listen to your children. They will have sudden and unexpected feelings like missing a brother or grandfather, even if the person has been dead for quite a while. These are real moments of grief, but they will be buried if children don't think you will understand.*

*Chapter 9*

# Their Curiosity, Our Pain?

*C*hildren are concerned about the necessities of life. Jeff wanted to know that his brother was being cared for. He wanted to know what he was wearing, if he had food, if he needed us to send his crib. My husband and I taught him about Jesus and heaven and the angels and all Justin's needs being supplied.

Shortly after Justin's death, Jeff and I were shopping when he was unusually attracted to a baby. Being an outgoing child, this was normal. But there was a strange attraction to this child. It went on so long and so passionately that I finally had to pull him away, making him say good-bye so we could continue our shopping and so the baby's mother could escape Jeff's grip.

As we started to leave, Jeff grabbed me and asked frantically, "Mom, Mom! Was that our Justin?"

Needless to say, this shopping spree ended abruptly and I sobbed all the way home. I was horrified! How could he think we had just given our baby to someone else?

The wise counsel of a friend helped me learn two important lessons from that incident: (1) His was a natural curiosity; the severe pang of grief was mine alone. Jeff was too young to understand the finality of death and the moral implications of just giving a child away. (2) That is what we had taught him. We had given our baby to Jesus. Through the eyes of a child, this kind lady pushing the stroller may have been Jesus . . . or Jesus' baby-sitter . . . or an angel. And maybe, just maybe, we were shopping in heaven.

Children are so full of questions. They are so cheerful in the way they ask. Every once in a while, however, they ask a question that pierces our own heart. Those are the tough times. Those are the times when we need to share tears rather than scoldings.

Realizing that most of Jeff's questions were the result of a natural curiosity about this unknown world created by recent deaths in his family helped me to cope with his endless questions that multiplied my grief because I read my emotions into him.

## How Does a Child Think?

Debi is a teacher and head of the women's ministry at her church. When her four-year-old son Adam asked her, "How do we go to heaven?" she was thrilled. She presented the four spiritual laws as they had never been taught before! Nothing could compare with the privilege of leading your own son to Christ.

After she finished, she asked Adam if he had any questions. He said, "Well, I was wondering if you could take an airplane, but it looks a little too high."

In general, children are concrete thinkers and live in the eternal now; today is an eternity, and today is all there is. Every morning their eyes shine as though they were seeing daylight for the first time. Understanding this helps us deal with the myriad and oft-repeated questions:

"When will he come back?"
"When can we go visit?"
"Does he have a crib?"
"When can we visit?"
"Where does he sleep?"
"When will he come back?"

"Who feeds him?"
"When can we visit?"
"Can I go give him his bottle?"
"When will he come back?"
"When can we go visit?"

## What Are a Child's Basic Reactions to Grief, Based on Personality?

Children's reactions to grief will closely parallel their basic personality style. If our child's personality is different from our personality, we may try to scold or correct him because we don't understand his reactions. If it is too much like our own personality, we may read our emotions and adult understanding into his words. We need to remember that whatever he says or does is evidence of his curiosity and understanding at the moment. How we react to his words and actions in times of grief is almost always borne of our personal pain.

The concept of personality differences is not new; Hippocrates named the four temperaments. Although I had read these principles from different sources, it was the work of Florence Littauer that made this information relevant and meaningful to me.[8] Of course, there are no two people in the world alike, and we all have both strengths and weaknesses. We approach life, learning, and loss, however, from one of four broad perspectives: sanguine, choleric, melancholy, and phlegmatic.

### Sanguine

The sanguine personality is the world's natural born cheerleader. Sanguines are friendly, optimistic, and outgoing. They inspire others to action and enthrall their audiences. Since a strength carried to excess becomes a weakness, sanguines in mourning may talk all the time and may have trouble facing the truth during a serious illness.

Grieving sanguine children have a tendency to close their eyes and pretend everything is okay. They may cry hysterically at a funeral but walk away and seem to forget that one they love has died. They may go on outwardly unaffected until something later in life triggers their buried grief. In times of sorrow they may tell sadistic jokes or exaggerate the truth: "All the cats in the neighborhood are dying," "Everyone I love disappears," etc. Sanguines especially have trouble with closure. They will respond well when asked to talk about their experience. Basically, they are people pleasers, and talking helps them, even if they are young children, to reflect on their loss and reach closure.

### Choleric

The choleric personality is the world's natural born leader. Cholerics are focused, goal oriented, and quick decision makers. They love to learn and need to be in control of their lives. Since a strength carried to excess becomes a weakness, cholerics in mourning may manipulate or threaten when they fear life is out of control.

Grieving children with choleric personalities have a tendency to place blame. They may be verbal about their anger—their anger at the person who died, for leaving them; their anger at those who remain, for being so stupidly sentimental; their anger at medical professionals, for not preventing the death; or their anger at God, for not intervening. In response to grief, cholerics tend to get busy and move on. They are the personality most likely to hide their grief by becoming workaholics. They have deep emotions but usually express them in doing rather than talking. They will respond well to getting involved in causes that represent the deceased, such as collecting donations for a children's hospital.

### Melancholy

The melancholy personality is the world's natural born organizer. Melancholies are detailed, compassionate, and perfectionistic. They always go the extra mile and strive to please. Since a strength carried to excess becomes a weakness, melancholies in mourning have a deep fear of failure. They endeavor to keep the family running and orderly. Because of their nature as caretakers, in times of stress their families may take advantage of them.

Mourning children with melancholy personalities may feel overburdened and powerless. Their own deep compassion often immobilizes them. They are the personality most prone to typical symptoms of depression. They respond well to writing about the deceased, drawing pictures, and talking quietly to one or two trusted friends.

### Phlegmatic

The phlegmatic personality is the world's natural born counselor. Phlegmatics are great listeners and mediators. They need peaceful relationships to be productive and happy. Since a strength carried to excess becomes a weakness, phlegmatics in mourning endeavor to make everyone happy and to restore peace in the family from the confusion brought on by a loss.

*It's okay to be there; it's not okay to stay.*

Our phlegmatic children concern themselves with the task of listening and waiting. They tend to live in a pretend world; the person who died often becomes their invisible friend. They will respond well to talking about their feelings; they will gain much from the nurturing they receive from just being allowed to listen and watch while funeral preparations are made. We need to make sure they are validated; they are so quiet at times that we can neglect them.

These are normal reactions. To an extent they are good, right, and healthy. When we have completed our grief work, we will operate out of the strengths of our personalities rather than out of the weaknesses. As we at Crystal Cathedral, in our grief recovery classes, watch the various personalities in mourning, we give them a slogan about their feelings and behavior: "It's okay to be there; it's not okay to stay."

---

*Recently a staff member moved to a better job. After she left, one of the kids kept asking, "When is she coming back from vacation?" This one child in particular didn't seem to understand. Our response was always the same: "She won't be coming back, because she works at a different place now." He would ask, "When is she coming back to see me?" This young boy appeared to be having trouble comprehending that the staff member's new job meant that she would no longer be working with us and couldn't come back to see us anymore. (In my line of work, returning to visit a child would be considered very unprofessional.) Over the course of time he would make little statements: "I hope that she is doing okay, because I miss her a lot." It was difficult for some staff to know how to respond, because they knew how close these two were. It was hard to determine if he really didn't understand what it meant for her to get a new job or if he was mourning the fact that she was no longer there. His questions appeared to be harder on the staff than on the child.*

*I remember wanting to go see Justin a lot when I was younger and not understanding why I couldn't. That's when I asked all the persistent questions I usually asked. I think it is highly necessary to humor the questions kids ask. More times than not they are merely speaking aloud exactly what they are thinking at that particular moment.*

## Chapter 10

# Should Children Attend the Services?

*W*e decided Jeff was too young to participate in his brother's memorial service, so we hired baby-sitters for him while the crowd that gathered to mourn accompanied us through the service. We later realized this had created a great deal of confusion for him. Children need a time to say good-bye, just as adults do.

Shortly after Justin's death we had a chance to see this in action. Jeff's grandfather passed away (death number four in our year of the big black cloud). We took Jeff to view his grandfather's body, explaining again that his spirit had left his body and that he now had a whole, new, healthy body in heaven.

Jeff began chattering away, talking to his grandpa's body: "Hi, Grandpa Wally. I came down to visit. Can you play with me?" After a few minutes of chatter he turned to me indignantly, exclaiming, "Mom! Grandpa Wally won't talk to me."

I again explained patiently that although Grandpa Wally's body was here, the part of him that we all loved, his spirit and soul, the part of him that walked, talked, and loved us, was in heaven with Jesus—and with Justin. What we were looking at was just the body he lived in while on earth. He didn't need it anymore because he was healthy and free of pain. Now he could see (Grandpa Wally was blind on earth).

*This helped clear the confusion Jeff had about Justin. We explained that Justin's spirit also had gone to heaven. Justin's body was in a grave because he too no longer needed it. His new body also was well.*

*Realizing that this confusion was normal helped us respond to Jeff's future questions for what they were: honest questions. It helped us not to confuse his attempt to understand with our pain.*

---

"They're so young."

"It will confuse them."

"They won't understand."

"It will frighten them."

We have so many reasons to exclude our children. But there are better reasons for involving them. Children can handle what they see and hear—truth is always our powerful ally—but they are confused and feel abandoned when they are excluded. The truth, the ritual, can't be more frightening than their vivid imaginations, especially when they see a host of family and friends dressed in black, wiping away tears, and putting feigned smiles on their faces.

## How Can We Encourage Our Children to Participate?

I interviewed both children and adults about their childhood experiences with death. Children at a very young age have strong feelings about whether or not they want to attend the ceremonies associated with death. Most of the adults I interviewed felt strongly that children should be made to go, if they themselves, as children, had begged to go to a loved one's memorial service and were excluded. Most of the adults I interviewed felt strongly that children should be given the dignity of choice, if they themselves, as children, hadn't wanted to attend services but were forced to. A few who had traumatic experiences as children felt that a young child should never attend a funeral.

Tim remembers attending his first funeral at age five. It was in a big, boxy church with hard pews. The women were hysterical, and he thought, *What's the big deal? It's just a funeral.* After the service they got food! As an adult, he still remembers it: ham, bologna, and zwieback. This is normal. Food is a very important thing in a little boy's life, especially before he discovers the wonders of cars and girls.

When Edie was five, the sweetest person in her whole life, her grandfather, died. Or maybe she was six. Her mind just won't remember. She wasn't allowed to attend the funeral or view his body. They thought her memory would be sullied or diminished by that experience. Although she has buried and mourned many loved ones over the years, she continues to mourn her grandfather almost fifty years later. Her parents loved her and thought they were protecting her. In reality they denied her closure, by which she could transform those memories from tragedy on earth to treasure in heaven. When we do our grief work and reach closure, the deep soul pain is assuaged but the love and memories remain.

> *Children at a very young age have strong feelings about whether or not they want to attend the ceremonies associated with death.*

Maria, age eight, was taken to a funeral where not one person spoke to her. No one hugged her or explained why they were there. She watched people throw themselves on the casket, wailing and screaming. She remembers this as one of two terrifying experiences from her childhood. She believes strongly in hugs, words, and explanations for children—and that they should never be forced to attend funeral services. When the children in her life must deal with grief, she will treat them much differently than she was treated.

Barbara's father died when she was nine. She was sent to stay with friends for a few days. She was allowed to see her father in the casket but did not attend the funeral. Today an adult, she still wishes she had been at the funeral to see a celebration of his life. He was a wonderful person.

Mindy, age ten, had twice attended the rituals of death. It wasn't until funeral number three, when she asked to kiss her great-grandpa, that she realized what death meant. Her daddy carried her out sobbing uncontrollably, but he sat with her, loving and hugging her and listening to her fears. It is a memory now but not a horrible one. She is able to talk naturally with her children about death.

Ronnie, age ten, was not allowed to go to his grandma's funeral. He cried for days, seemingly inconsolable. He awoke one morning aglow. "Grandma," he said, "came to my room last night and told me she loved me and would always be there for me." His parents were shocked and distraught over the sudden death of their mother, so God had to take care of this one!

All these people had different journeys of understanding, but from the interviews the following generalities were gleaned.

- Children should be encouraged, but not forced, to participate. If they opt not to attend the ceremonies, make sure they have a special time alone with close family members to say good-bye to their loved one.
- If children want to participate, someone who isn't overly emotional should tell them ahead of time exactly what to expect. This should include *what* will happen, *where* the service will take place, *when* they will move from one place to

another, *who* will be there, *how* various people may react (tears, wailing, etc.), and *why* we have these ceremonies of death. No, they won't understand everything, and yes, you will have to explain it again, but they will remember it more positively if an adult shows them this respect.

- Some loving adult not overburdened by his or her own grief should accompany the children during the service.
- After the service a caring adult should ask the children if they have any questions.
- We should remember that attending the services doesn't mean understanding the impact of death. That will take time.

The ceremonies of death are as varied as the ceremonies of life. Whatever is your custom, allow but don't force your children to participate in it. If they are old enough to express an opinion, let them decide whether or not to go to the services. Allow them to experience the rituals of mourning. Allow them to ask their questions. Patiently explain to them about our body being the house we live in temporarily.

The reality of seeing a dead body can't be worse than the images their active imaginations conjure up, especially when they have Hollywood and Halloween for fuel. Their experience of grief is far healthier and easier to deal with than their feelings of abandonment caused by the confusion going on around them while they are excluded from conversations and events.

## How Do We Respond to the Heart of Our Children's Questions?

If we can remove ourselves emotionally from the situation, our children's comments and questions will help us help them. If we react emotionally instead, we create confusion in them.

When viewing his grandmother in the casket, eight-year-old Jared asked, "Does she have any legs?" He could only see her from the chest up. He was asking out of curiosity, not out of sorrow. To these questions we respond with facts: "Her legs are under this lid. Her body is all here but her spirit is in heaven."

When children draw pictures of ghosts and ask questions about flying spirits, they may really be asking about separation of spirit and body.

When you overhear them telling a friend that they went to heaven last night, they may really be wondering how eternity transcends time and space.

When they draw pictures obsessed with violence or in dreary colors, they may be angry; perhaps they're asking why and questioning the purpose of life.

When they tell morbid jokes, they may really be asking why death would visit *their* family and not that of a friend.

When they create an imaginary friend, they may be dealing with closure and wondering how to build a bridge between heaven and earth.

Until children understand what it means to die, their questions will be those of curiosity. Once they understand death, their reactions may be emotional. As they mature and grow in a healthy environment, their intellect and their emotions can coexist. Until then patiently love them, talk to them, and answer their questions.

## How Do We Help Our Children Say Good-bye?

Children develop fears associated with the unknown. When we try to protect them from death or illness by sending them outside to play or away to visit friends, it is often because we don't want to frighten them. We think they might be afraid of death if we expose them too early.

Our good intentions backfire on us. Children become afraid of death because they don't understand what is happening. They see people crying and rushing and hushing and don't know why. They hear it's because of death but they don't know what death is. Someone who was special to them no longer comes around. When our children ask to visit the deceased, we smile and tell them he or she is in heaven. But the smile we wear for our children carries a body language that defies happiness, leaving them confused. They don't know where heaven is. People tell them the one they love is all well now, but he or she can't play anymore. The person will never return, but no one thought to give the children a chance to say good-bye.

We hear it often: "A funeral is not for the dead but for the living." We adults gather after one we love has died. We gather to remember; we gather to say those things we weren't able to say in life; we gather for support to get through life as it will be, forever altered because of our new circumstance. In short, we gather for closure. We say good-bye to a past that will always be a part of us. Until we do that, we can't carve out our future. When our loved ones tell us not to have a funeral—"Don't cry for me"; "Send me the flowers now"; "I don't want a sad service with people looking at me"—their intentions are good. We should express our love to the living. But not to say good-bye causes us to be forever indebted to the person who died; we never let go.

> *No one thought to give the children a chance to say good-bye.*

If we don't find closure, we may carry our loss into our relationships. Every time someone gets too close, we end the relationship and move on. Dan, at age thirty-six, is finally ready to break that cycle. He spent last Father's Day at the grave of his father. He went there not to find his father, who had died thirty years before, but, in his words, "to find the Dan that was dying while still living."

Whether or not they attend the ceremonies, your children need to say good-bye. Make this a formal time within a few months of the death. Do something special in memory of the person who died. Drawing a picture for or about Grandma, writing a letter to or about Uncle Harry, or telling a beloved pet or doll about the person who died are normal ways for children (and adults) to reach closure. If they do not reach closure in a relationship, that loss will haunt them. I spend many hours at women's retreats, counseling those who have never said good-bye.

You can give your children a great gift. Give them their heritage now rather than having them wait thirty years to find it.

In our grief recovery program at the Crystal Cathedral, we have our participants write a good-bye letter. They say everything they didn't get a chance to say. They ask God to get the message across. Then we have a letting-go ceremony. We write the names of those we love on balloons. We color code the balloons; each participant chooses a color that expresses what they need to say. Those in deep depression take a black balloon. It symbolizes, "This is the hardest thing I've ever had to do. If I had any other option, I would take it. Since I don't, I'm letting go . . . but I will never forget." Those who are angry (and children are often angry) take a red balloon. It stands for, "I'm letting go, but God will get you for leaving me!" A yellow balloon is for those ready to begin life again: "A part of me will always love you, but with God's help I'm moving on." And for all of us in Christ, a white balloon is necessary. It means, "Till we meet again." As we let go, we ceremoniously repeat the serenity prayer:

*God, grant me the serenity to accept the things I cannot change,*
*The courage to change the things I can,*
*And the wisdom to know the difference.*

Participants say this is both the hardest and the most healing session we have. You can have a private ceremony with your children. Yours can also involve a symbolic balloon, one that has special meaning just for you.

There are two things I feel strongly about: (1) everyone should have the right to choose how they express their grief, and (2) children are hurt if they don't reach closure. I know these can coexist, but every family will have to decide how.

---

*How do you tell a young child about death? Children don't seem to totally grasp all the abstract concepts that adults do. I have found, though, that if you tell a young child that God took the person who died, that will cause some unnecessary anger at God. But do not let the fear of angering your child cause you to sugarcoat the truth. Anger is a very normal and important part of life. Children need to be taught ways to appropriately handle their anger, even when it is directed at God.*

*I remember going to see Wally's body. I don't remember talking to him, although I do remember the viewing. I remember thinking for some reason that Justin's coffin was underneath Wally's, behind the curtain draped beneath Wally's coffin so as to not let us see it. I was kind of mad that nobody understood what I was talking about, and I wondered why nobody would lift up the curtain below Wally's casket.*

*It is very important for a child, no matter how young, to be allowed to attend a funeral service. Children may not understand all the reasons for everyone's sadness, but it will help them understand death in a more realistic and honest way. I think many times parents create a false concept of death. Parents make it seem as if God took the dead person on vacation to Florida and that's where heaven is. If you allow children to go to a funeral, it will help them grasp the permanence of death and begin the healing process.*

*I remember going up to Fresno alone one summer—it was while I was in college, I think—to visit Justin's gravesite just for my own little personal trip. I had quite a good cry that day and a good chat with my brother. I think that day was me finally getting to have a funeral service of my own for my brother. There wasn't anyone else around, so I didn't have to feel I had to comfort anyone and be the strong one. It was just me being able to let myself cry and say good-bye to my brother. The next time I visited his gravesite, it wasn't a sad event at all. It was almost as if I had just gone over to his house and visited with him for a while.*

## Chapter 11

# To Remember or to Forget?

*When Jeff was twelve, our church invited him to play in a golf tournament. Normally he would have been ecstatic, but he told me he wasn't going to play.*

*That was not normal behavior for the boy who begged everyone, always, to take him golfing. Knowing something wasn't right, I began asking probing questions.*

*His response: "Mom, I can't. It's on Justin's birthday."*

*I quickly responded, "Oh, Jeff, Justin would want you to go! Hit a ball in his honor!"*

*Jeff went, and that began our yearly ritual of remembering: every April 1, rain or shine, we play a game of golf in honor of a wonderful brother and son who, I'm sure, looks on us from heaven. He probably cheers when Jeff hits the ball, and laughs hysterically at his mother!*

*Perhaps Justin hits a ball in our honor as well. You never know!*

---

Serving a birthday cake and having a party for Justin was so unnatural. In fact, it was hypocritical. It was the saddest little party I've ever attended. The intention was right; the ritual was wrong. A game of golf in our family, however, speaks love! We have found our right celebration.

## Should Children Remember or Forget?

Should we help our children remember the person who died, or should we help them forget and get on with their lives?

By all means, remember! By all means, love life and move on! The two coexist. One makes the other more glorious.

If we don't help our children remember, their imagined memories will control them. We have watched people whose life was damaged because of such memories. We watch as children remember a perfect father, remember in such a way that they can never allow a surrogate or stepparent into their hearts, remember in such a way that they can never be a perfect father and thus their own parenting suffers. We watch as children remember the perfect brother or sister and wish they had died instead because they can never be good. Yes, we need to remember, but we need to remember the real person; we need to remember in truth.

> *By all means, remember! By all means, love life and move on! The two coexist. One makes the other more glorious.*

I interviewed my grandmother for her eighty-ninth birthday. My grandpa had died a few years earlier, and suddenly I was filled with questions I would never be able to ask. I didn't want that to happen with Gram, so I decided that in honor of her birthday, I would give her other family members the gift of memories. During the interview my saintly and wonderful grandma responded with incredible answers. I soaked them up. But after a while I said, "You're not even human. Didn't you ever do anything bad?" I learned of her burning down her father's barn and feeding the preacher's son chicken pellets. She was a saintly woman but she was also a mischievous one. What a sad thing if we had left out the piece that made her Gram!

The person who died is a part of our heritage. God intended that we remember; God intended that those who have gone before us show us by their example the way to heaven. God intended us to know a little of his love by having loved one another. God intended that we see people as human beings with needs and shortcomings who are loved for who they are, not for who they should be. God intended that we know the pain of separation. How else could we conceive of a God whose love is greater, a God who forgives and restores, a God whose heart is broken and lonely when we stray?

## How Do We Help Our Children Remember?

Riding to nursery school one morning, Amber, age five, told her mother, "Aunt Marjorie is not gone. She is still right there inside my head. And whenever she starts to go away, I just say, 'You get right back in there!'"

*Spontaneous comments and events trigger a memory.* Laugh with your children about something funny the one who died did or said. Have them share a memory with a friend. Take them to the gravesite on special occasions. Sometimes talking about things at the gravesite helps us clarify our thinking. Send off a balloon or a bottle with a special message inside. Eat at the loved one's favorite restaurant. Cook his or her favorite meal and talk about the person. Look at old pictures.

*We remember through causes.* As a family, adopt a needy child for Christmas in memory of the one who is gone. Volunteer in a hospital, hospice, or rest home. Continue a cause that the loved one started. Collect for a charity that supports research about, or helps people with, a similar affliction.

*We remember on special days and by observing certain rituals.* We might set aside a specific time that is devoted to memory. For

Jeff and me it is Justin's birthday. For some it is an anniversary or holiday.

I have another ritual, one that is mine alone. Every April I, usually late in the evening, I spend time reflecting on the child I love who is being raised in heaven rather than on earth. I write him a letter. I think about what life would be like were he here. Would he be getting his driver's license? Having his first date? I tell him the mother things I need to say. I cry. I always cry. It's sad my son isn't here, even though it's joyful he's healthy and whole and free of pain in heaven.

And I wonder. I wonder if he's still an infant or if people grow and mature in heaven. I wonder if he's a golfer. I wonder if he's musical—I always thought he would be. I wonder if he's giving Grandma a rough time and a lot of boy hugs. I know he would if they were here!

In short, I imagine heaven as I reflect. Heaven has always been a wonderful place in my mind and heart. Now it's even more awesome and personal. My son lives there.

Jeff knows about this ritual now. Occasionally he writes me a letter at the time I am writing to Justin.

Our rituals help us remember in a healthy way that we have a treasure in heaven. They help us deal with our ongoing grief, reprioritize our lives, and cry the tears that have been building up without warning since last we took the time to reflect.

Creating a ritual for remembering helps our children express their questions and concerns. Once when we were talking, Jeff wanted to go see Justin. I told him Justin was in heaven, so we couldn't go until we died. He said, "No, I want to go see the other Justin, the one in the ground." I didn't know he was still struggling with the concept of separation of body and spirit. That reminded me to help him understand.

There is another reason to remember, one that is vital to our children's self-concept. If we could forget one who died, we could forget them. Take time to remember so your children will know that they too are precious to you; you will *always* love them, and you could *never* forget them; you hurt when they hurt; you cry when they cry; you worry when they're not home. They matter!

---

*The process of developing rituals to remember people who have died is a tough one to figure out. You must find something that works for you, which at times can be as difficult as understanding death itself. I remember playing in this golf tournament, and once I got through the day, thinking to myself, Okay, I need to do this all the time on Justin's birthday. It turned out pretty well over all. I had a good golfing day, and I won a sand wedge that I didn't have in my bag yet. I still always manage to need that club whenever I get into a sand trap, which is often. So at least once or twice a round I pull out that golf club and think, Hey, I remember where I got this and kind of smile to myself.*

*Even though the golf club is merely a token, it helps me remember that my brother and I one day will be together. It reminds me that there is hope. It is incredibly important to help children remember those who have died. I think that without that remembrance, a part of their heritage will die. Remembering will help the healing process.*

*Chapter 12*

# How Do We Pray?

*This is perhaps the hardest story for me to share. I failed my son. I would like to pretend this didn't happen. If I do, you might make the same mistake I did.*

*It was during one of those nightmare seasons. Jeff had awakened me in the middle of the night—again. This had been going on for what seemed like forever.*

*When I stumbled into his room and held him, I asked him once again what was wrong. He began sobbing, "I want my Justin and I want my Daddy."*

*Not knowing what else to do, I suggested he pray about it. He sobbed, "Dear God, please bring back my Justin and please bring back my Daddy."*

*I intellectualized. I said, "Jeff, you can't pray like that! God can't bring back our Justin. He's dead. And God can't bring back Daddy unless Daddy chooses to come home. God can only change a willing heart."*

*Somehow we made it through the night, sobbing together, but I was haunted by my words. I kept thinking, That's the truth, so why does it feel so awful?*

*Fortunately, I was in counseling at the time; our horrible year had taken a great toll on us all. I shared my experience with the therapist. He said, "You told him what?"*

*I repeated my words: "You can't pray like that . . ."*

*He responded, "But he wasn't praying to you."*

*We can and should encourage our children to pour out their honest heart cries to God.*

The answer to the question of how to pray seems so obvious. It isn't. In guiding our children in prayer, we instill some very damaging concepts. We edit; we critique; we explain. Instead we should open the doorway to God with their honest confusion. He can speak to children; he doesn't need our help.

When we are broken, angry, and grieving, we pour out our honest heart cries to God. We beg; we complain; we cry; we pout; we bargain; we judge; we ask for vengeance; we tell him life isn't fair; we suggest who should be hurting instead of us; we tell him how pious and worthy we are.

## How Can We Help Our Children Pray?

We can and should encourage our children to pour out their honest heart cries to God. When their cries touch our pain, we feel our pain and pour out our honest heart cries to God. We don't edit, correct, scold, or suggest.

In the delightful book *Children's Letters to God*, we have a great example of this type of prayer. Little Jane asks,

Dear God,

Instead of letting people die and having to make new ones, why don't you just keep the ones you got now?[9]

When we interfere with our children's prayers, we block their channel to heaven. We step between them and God. We short-circuit his ability to comfort them and become their loving heavenly Father. We don't want to do that! They'll need him all their lives.

Tammie and David helped their daughter talk to God. After her great-great-grandma, who was also her best friend, died,

Elizabeth's bedtime prayers changed from precious times with God to resentful, ugly talks to God. So many times they wanted to stop her. In their minds they screamed, *He's God! You can't talk to him that way.* But each evening they felt the Holy Spirit stop them from scolding her for her irreverence. *He is God,* the Spirit seemed to say. *He already knows how she's feeling. Just let her talk with him about her troubles.*

After several frustrating weeks of tears and awful prayers, they were awakened one morning by the sound of little feet running through the house at top speed. Elizabeth burst through their door. With a beaming smile on her face, she said, "I saw Grandma. She's with Jesus and she's happy. It's white there, and there's music and flowers and Grandma's happy!"

She still misses Grandma, but the agony of the separation disappeared that day.

Was it real? A vision? A dream? Whatever form it took, it was God loving one of his children. I still hurt when I realize that I cheated my son out of the gift of communication with God.

---

*I learned how to pray from several different people—little tidbits from each, nothing too terribly profound from any one of them—but when I finally learned to put all the tidbits together, my prayer life dramatically changed. I didn't realize it had changed until I was in college. I was home for a summer and involved in a college group through my church. We started one evening sharing concerns we all had. Everyone had been having a really hard time with life. I was asked to pray, so I did. I started the prayer, "Dear God. Right now life stinks...." I don't remember the rest of the prayer. One of my friends in the room later talked to me and told me how cool it was that I was so blunt with God. The general feeling is that you aren't supposed to be so direct with God. At the time that was all I could think of that fit. Things were awful for everyone there.*

*Every so often one of my friends, now a youth pastor, and I get together for lunch. We reminisced the other day about that prayer, and he uses that particular phrase whenever he talks to his kids about prayer.*

*Brutal honesty with God—that is my way of praying. Help your children to let God know how they feel. Encourage them to be willing to allow God to work through their grief with them, but tell them they need to openly share their feelings with him. That way not only are they being honest with God, they are being honest with themselves.*

# *Part 3*

## Tough Questions Children Ask

*As Justin's condition began to deteriorate and we realized he might not make it, I lamented one night to our doctor that Jeff wasn't able to be a part of his brother's life. We would periodically take him to the outside hospital window where he could touch the glass while we held Justin up to it. It was better than leaving him home with a baby-sitter, but it seemed so cold and impersonal.*

*Dr. Bonner quickly responded with a written order to the nurses: "Allow Jeff to go to Justin's room." Thankfully, he realized we had an entire family who were mourning. So many people, during an illness, forget about the children.*

*The nurses were instructed to not notice that a child was inside the corridors. Imagine how difficult it was for the nurses to ignore Jeff when he, animated, stopped each one we passed to say, "I get to go see my brother today. I don't have to look at him through the window. I get to hold him. I don't have to watch through the window today. I get to hold my brother. I'm going to my brother's room. I don't have to watch through the window."*

We did a better job of preparing Jeff for Justin's death than we did answering his questions and guiding him after it happened. We kept him informed and as much a part of the process as hospital policy allowed. Justin's death, although not understood, was not a surprise to him.

We were lucky. As painful as it was, we were warned. We knew Justin's death was imminent. We had a chance to say goodbye. Jeff had a chance to say good-bye. We had watched Justin suffer so much that we were willing to let him go. It was gut-wrenching, and we questioned everything we had always said we believed about heaven. But in the end we could let our baby slip into the arms of Jesus, where he wouldn't ever have to suffer again. We could do that because we knew we would see him again someday in a grand and heavenly reunion. We could do that because we do not "grieve like the rest of men, who have no hope" (I Thessalonians 4:13).

Some people faced with death aren't as fortunate. They don't have a warning. They don't have the opportunity or ability to say good-bye. Some believe good-bye is forever.

Either way, those with children must face death in a very different way than they would alone. When children learn about death, they are full of questions. If they aren't asking you questions, they may be mulling them over in their minds, or they may have learned that questions hurt you, so they are talking with someone else. Both of these are okay and healthy. When they bury their questions so deeply that they don't talk and try not to even think about it, they need help.

There are the typical questions: "Where is heaven?" "When will he come back?" Children ask them. The questions they don't ask are just as real. They are covered in the next section. This section will deal with the never-ending stream of questions children ask as we endeavor to explain to them the unexplainable: heaven, death, and eternity.

———————

*The only time I remember getting to hold my brother was during one of the quite brief periods when he was home. He and I were having our pictures made together. I remember him sleeping most of the time; I kept trying to wake him up, but with no success. I remember wanting him to play with me. I dashed through the living room yelling, "Hey, Justin, let's go play some football!" and then proceeded out the front door as fast as I could run. A moment later I came back in saying, "Hey, Justin, what's taking so long?" I was only three and didn't understand that he was neither healthy enough nor old enough to catch and throw a ball.*

*Those snapshots I have always had and will always carry with me.*

*The child at work who couldn't understand our staff member leaving asked questions we didn't anticipate and didn't quite know how to handle, such as "Did she leave because she doesn't like me any more?" We adults understood that she had taken the new job because it was a good career move, but it's tough to explain that to a young boy. His questions were laced with guilt, confusion, and childish thinking. We needed to answer his immediate questions factually, but we also needed to watch for opportunities to help him deal with his guilt.*

*Be prepared for questions you have no idea how to answer. Children will ask them. Especially remember these two words: listen and love.*

*Chapter 13*

# What Happens When You Die?

*Justin's life and death was a time when God was real and ever present in spite of circumstances.*

*Leading up to his death, we got many calls from the hospital telling us he might not make it. One week while Jeff was running a dangerously high fever, we got three calls from the hospital telling us that Justin was not expected to live through the day. What a dilemma! Do we leave a seriously ill Jeff to be at Justin's bedside? Do we leave our Justin to die alone? Should one of us go and one stay home? Which one? It was agonizing.*

*The day Justin died wasn't like that. Jeff was well. He had just celebrated his third birthday. He was playing at the home of one of his best buddies, Ty. Justin was stable, medically speaking, but we knew we needed to be there. No one had to tell us; we just knew.*

*His death . . . that's another story. God was there. Joe Bayly expresses my sentiments in his book* The Last Thing We Talk About: *"I cannot explain it, but my wife and I have never been more convinced of His love for us and our children than when we have turned from a fresh grave."[10]*

*We called Ty's parents, who were also our friends, to let them know, and they graciously emptied their living room for us to spend some time alone with Jeff, easing him into the news.*

*"Jeff, our Justin died today."*

*Death was not a stranger to him, in spite of his young age. Gammy, his grandma, and Daboy, his great-grandfather, had just died. I don't recall that he said anything in response, so we continued.*

*"You know how he was very sick. Well, now he's all well. He's in heaven with Jesus. He doesn't hurt anymore. He's with Gammy and Daboy. He's all well. We'll miss him, but we're happy he's okay."*

---

Although heaven was no stranger to Jeff, heaven was a mystery. If I had known then what I know now, perhaps I would have done a better job of explaining the death of his brother. Perhaps I would have explained what it means to die. Certainly I would have included him in the memorial service.

## What Do Children Say?

My grandmother was supposed to die when I was about five years old. Her family had gathered at her bedside. Suddenly she sat up, saying, "Oh, do you see them? Do you see them?" She could see the wings of angels leaving her bed. I grew up with that story. Gram was very pragmatic but not when she spoke of the angels. I never questioned whether they were real; I knew when I looked at her.

One day when I was in college, I begged her, "Gram, paint the angels for me."

She replied, "Oh, I can't. They don't have colors like that on earth. The wings were every color of the rainbow, but they were brighter. They had a glow. We don't have anything that beautiful here. Our colors just couldn't do it justice."

The Bible tells us, "No eye has seen, no ear has heard, no mind has conceived what God has prepared for those who love him" (I Corinthians 2:9). The best that we can imagine can't compare to the awesome heaven that awaits us and is home for those we love. Allow children to explore the mysteries of heaven and death. Have them draw pictures of heaven and of the home their brother, mother, grandpa, or aunt now lives in. Let them write letters to or draw pictures for the deceased. Help them pray that God will give their loved ones their letters and tell them they are missed and loved. Let our children imagine how wonderful and beautiful a place heaven must be. Let them imagine what happens as we make this transition from earth to heaven. As we listen to their words, we will know how to help them find peace, and we'll be planting the seeds of eternity in their hearts.

Before being diagnosed with a terminal brain stem tumor, five-year-old Grace talked with her parents about heaven and what she could take in her coffin. Her mother realizes now that God was both preparing Grace for heaven and using Grace to prepare her parents for the news that their daughter would die young.

Zachary, age six, says, "Sunday is God's special day. So on Sundays God wakes up, finds all the good people who have died that week, and takes them to heaven with him. So if you die on Sunday, be sure it's early in the morning, before God wakes up, or you have to wait until the next Sunday to go to heaven."

Suzanne, age six, told her mother, "My Palm Springs Grandpa had two lives." When asked what she meant, she replied, "First on earth and now in heaven with Jesus."

Ann was nine when her daddy died. She remembers everyone crying at his memorial service, but she couldn't understand why. She pinched herself very hard so she could cry, too. She felt she ought to cry but she didn't know why. Looking back, she didn't realize that death was final. She was too young for that, but someone could have explained the tears to her so she could have begun to acknowledge her own emotions.

Fran remembers attending a funeral with her grandmother at age three. Most of what she remembers is people fanning themselves. She wanted to use a fan, and no one offered to share one with her! Her next memory of understanding death is at age twelve, saying her prayers at night and pleading with God not to let her die. Fears are normal, especially when we have the media to feed our subconscious; bad dreams and desperate prayers tell us our children need reassurance.

Karen was fourteen when two of her best friends were electrocuted. At this age she knew death was final. She did two very healing things: she cried until she could cry no more; then she shared funny stories about them with other friends, and they laughed themselves silly. Tears and laughter are very closely related. They both cleanse us from deep soul pain. Deep soul pain is normal in the aftermath of death.

## How Can We Help Our Children Understand?

We can use the familiar to teach the unfamiliar.

*Draw from past experiences.* "You remember how we moved from our old house into our new house? Well, in a way our body is the house where our spirit lives. Your body is the part of you that has blond hair and blue eyes. That's the house for your spirit. Your spirit is the part of you that laughs and cries and dreams and loves. When you die, your spirit leaves your earthly body-house, and you get a new house in heaven. Your new body will never get sick or hurt again. That's where Auntie Lou is now. She moved out of this house, and she has a new house where her spirit lives, in heaven."

*Use nature.* "See this pretty butterfly? It was once a pretty caterpillar. Then it went into a cocoon and came out as a butterfly. That's a little bit like it is when we die. We change from our earthly bodies, like the caterpillar, into a new body we get in heaven, like the butterfly. We're still the same inside, but we're not limited to things like gravity, and we're not hurt by things like skinned knees or cancer anymore."

*Use relationships.* "Remember how excited you were to go spend a week with Grandma last summer? Remember how much fun you had but how we missed each other? Well, Grandma was just as excited to get to spend eternity with Jesus and with her mommy and daddy. She is okay and happy there even though we miss her."

## What Does the Bible Say?

*God is with our loved ones as they leave this earth. They are safe, they are with him, and they are not afraid.* "Even though I walk through the valley of the shadow of death, I will fear no evil, for you are with me; your rod and your staff, they comfort me" (Psalm 23:4). Especially when death involves another child, the remaining children want to know that the person who died didn't just wander away lost but was indeed being guided by the Good Shepherd.

*Those we love are alive in heaven.* "Jesus said to her, 'I am the resurrection and the life. He who believes in me will live, even though he dies'" (John 11:25). Children need to think of death as a transition from this life into the next one rather than as an end to life on earth.

*Those we love are resting and at peace. They don't hurt anymore.* "Those who walk uprightly enter into peace; they find rest as they lie in death" (Isaiah 57:2). Resting is more appealing to an adult than to a child, but knowing that those who died are at peace and happy in heaven is a comfort to children. They worry about little things like where Grandpa is sleeping if he isn't in his bed and who is feeding him if he isn't eating with Grandma anymore. They worry that he may still be sick in heaven but have no one to take care of him.

*Our loved ones have a reward in heaven.* "Now there is in store for me the crown of righteousness, which the Lord, the righteous Judge, will award to me on that day—and not only to me, but also to all who have longed for his appearing" (2 Timothy 4:8). Let children know that heaven is a place where their loved ones are happy and healthy and all their needs are supplied. They have a good home, and they are with a lot of their friends who died earlier.

*Christ destroyed the fear of death.* "Since the children have flesh and blood, he too shared in their humanity so that by his death he might destroy him who holds the power of death—that is, the devil—and free those who all their lives were held in slavery by their fear of death" (Hebrews 2:14–15). Tell your children that we don't need to be afraid to die. Uncle Joe wasn't afraid, because he knew he was going to be with Jesus.

*They can't come back, but we can someday go to them.* "I will go to him, but he will not return to me" (2 Samuel 12:23). Children need to know that death is final. Young children will have a hard time grasping this concept, but we need to plant seeds.

Remember too that children will grasp the concept of death just as they grasp all concepts—a little at a time, with you as their role model. As they grow, they will need to revisit these thoughts. Especially at transition times in their lives, they will reprocess what happened, assimilate the facts of loss into their new and more sophisticated minds. Their questions aren't usually based in deep pain; they are more often questions of curiosity.

## What Do Children Want and Need to Know?

*They need to know the difference between real and pretend.* The entertainment industry has given us both gruesome and celestial images of death. Questions are triggered in response to movies, television programs, video and computer games, and web sites. Especially in autumn it is common to see a dead person on some TV show get up in shadow form and hover around earth for a while. Witches and boiling pots abound, fueling our imagination. We parents need to help our children separate make-believe from real, and we need to carefully censor everything they watch. If they watch a frightening or thought-provoking movie, we need to watch it with them so we can recognize their reactions and talk them through their fears. The younger the child, the quicker we need to point out pretend: "In real life when we run over someone, they don't peel themselves off the pavement and get up again."

*They need to know that death is not to be feared.* Jesus died to conquer death. Because he rose again, we don't need to be afraid. When children are mourning, however, they usually are fearful, so we need to help them handle their fear. Since fear isn't intellectual, it can't be dealt with intellectually. When we help our children express their fear without shame, they usually can let it go. Often, being able to express it in words and being reassured of our love is all they need.

*They need to be told the truth.* Children, especially ages nine through twelve, have a great fascination with the gory details of death. They want to know exactly what happened. This begins their preteen fascination with burps and other bodily functions.

They may annoy us with their tasteless comments and questions. Remember that this is normal. Remember that they get gory details from television, movies, and friends. Children can handle the truth, and it can't be worse than what their imaginations conjure up. Be the person who tells them the truth, however painful, about both the death and the illness leading up to it:

> "Grandpa had emphysema caused by smoking when he was younger. That means that his lungs didn't work anymore. He couldn't breathe to get oxygen."
>
> "Grandma has cancer and it is in her brain. She doesn't know what she is saying, and our Grandma would never talk like that otherwise. Please forgive her and remember the person she was before she got sick."
>
> "When we die, our body slowly shuts down. Usually people can hear us even when they can't talk or respond. When you talk in Uncle Joe's room, talk to him but don't talk about him unless it is to say words of love."

*They need to know that God is there, caring for the person who dies.* Psalm 116:15 says, "Precious in the sight of the LORD is the death of his saints." Although we don't want to die and we may fear the process, God is in it. He is ministering to those we love when they don't seem to know or understand us. As they approach death, those who love God appear to be aware of two worlds, our world and the world of the spirit. It is common for them to talk with those who have previously died. Is this real or a hallucination? I don't know. But it is of God when it comforts them and helps their transition into heaven. We may be afraid of the illness or accident that leads to death, but we need not be afraid of the journey, "for you are with me; your rod and your staff, they comfort me" (Psalm 23:4).

## What Is Normal Behavior As Children Try to Understand?

*It is normal for children to mirror our behavior.* If you find your children avoiding mention of the deceased or acting extremely unemotional, look at yourself. Are you burying your tears? If your children can't seem to focus and get on with life, look back a few weeks. How have you been doing in that department? Remember that you are their role model.

*It is normal for children to tell morbid jokes.* The saying "ashes to ashes and dust to dust" fascinates them. They enjoy looking under a chair at a dust pile and saying things like, "There goes another one!" These not-so-funny jokes are normal as long as they don't last too long. We can gently teach them about good taste at these times.

*It is normal for children to be afraid they will die, too.* Listen to their symptoms and reassure them; don't scold them or ignore their fears.

*It is normal for children to eavesdrop, searching for answers.* When Steve's daughter was four, they thought she was too young to be exposed to the viewing of her grandmother at the funeral. A great aunt kept her in the background during the viewing and at the gravesite. Just after they left the cemetery, Elisa suddenly and innocently asked, "Mommy, Daddy, what was Grandma doing in the jewelry box?"

In this precious parenting moment they told her, "That's what you put them in when you send them to heaven." They couldn't have found a better illustration than the one she came up with!

*It is normal for children to think about events and draw conclusions.* That is why we need to listen much more than we talk. Using pets to teach about death is a wonderful thing to do, but sometimes it backfires! When Kimberly's hamster died, her parents put Hamlet into a little box and had a service. Kimberly and her friend Amy talked about how sweet he had been and how they would miss him. It was a beautiful and memorable event. When the service was over, Kimberly's father placed him in the trash can.

A few weeks later Kimberly's grandmother went to heaven. Her parents overheard Amy and Kimberly talking in the backseat of the car. Amy asked Kimberly if they were putting her grandma into a trash can, too. They took advantage of this teachable moment to help the girls understand. Imagine how confusing and frightening it would have been for both children if Kimberly's parents had not been listening, had failed to respond positively to their misunderstanding, or had shamed them.

*A big hug and being allowed to be sad is more powerful than anything ever said.*

---

*Most of what I learned about death came from watching my extended family at funerals. The family, which is quite large, has been very close. When I was between the ages of three and thirteen, there were a significant number of deaths in the family, and I attended the services.*

*My grandmother died when I was thirteen. As a part of being able to find some closure, I asked to be a pallbearer at her funeral. It was one last thing I could do for my grandmother, and it was an expression of love that went beyond any words.*

*I learned that words, no matter how well intended they are, don't comfort me. I learned that a big hug and being allowed to be sad is more powerful than anything ever said. For someone to simply be there with a shoulder to cry on is a godsend. Please make sure that you and your children are surrounded by loving, nurturing people throughout life. That way when death strikes, you will already have a support team to comfort you.*

## Chapter 14

# When Can I Go to Heaven to Visit?

*Jeff's grandma died when he was two and a half. Shortly after her death, his grandpa needed some time away, so he visited relatives in Texas. Jeff would walk up to total strangers in a store and announce excitedly, "Pappy's in Texas. Gammie's in heaven." The strangers looked a little shocked. Usually they would walk away from him without speaking.*

*To him it was logical. In response we told him that when people go to heaven, we can go to them but they cannot come to us. Pappy would be home soon but Gammy could never come back.*

*We shouldn't have been surprised, then, in the aftermath of Justin's death a few months later, that Jeff's sense of logic included travel. He would ask, then he would demand, "When can I go to heaven to visit my brother?" If we could visit Pappy in Texas, why not Gammy and Justin in heaven? If not a visit, how about a phone call? If heaven is a place, it must be a lot like Arizona or Hawaii or Los Angeles. We could drive or fly or take a bus—maybe even a boat.*

---

When our children excitedly ask this question, our hearts ache. If they go to heaven, they have to die. Death has been too recent a guest in our home for us not to cringe at this question.

If we can move beyond our emotional reaction, we can use this very teachable moment to instill in our children a desire to go to heaven when they die.

## What Does the Bible Say?

John 3:16 says, "God so loved the world that he gave his one and only Son, that whoever believes in him shall not perish but have eternal life." Therefore we can tell our children, "If we believe in Jesus, we will go to heaven when we die."

Revelation 3:20 says, "Here I am! I stand at the door and knock. If anyone hears my voice and opens the door, I will go in and eat with him, and he with me." Thus we can tell our children, "Jesus wants us to go to heaven. We need to listen for his voice and let him in. When our heart tells us to do good, that is God's voice speaking."

## What Can We Do Now?

*Keep a healthy memory alive.* When they ask about going to heaven, encourage them to remember the person who died. Balloons or toys taken to the grave of a loved one help our children say good-bye. Often our children will invent invisible friends who are much like a loved one who has recently died. This is normal and helps them through the grieving process. Remembering that someone in heaven loves you helps you make good decisions. Kyle, age eleven, says that sometimes when he is tempted to do something wrong, he remembers that his great-grandmother is in heaven and would know. With that to strengthen him, he can choose to do what is right.

Jean Paul Richter says, "Each departed friend is a magnet that attracts us to the next world."

*Anticipate and answer their questions.* Before Carol's mother died, she had visions of the family's children in heaven. One of them she described as a little blondish-brunette girl. Carol commented, "I've always wondered what color my sister's hair was." Carol was a mother herself when this happened. Only God knew of Carol's curiosity; she had never asked. Children are curious about those who died, even those who died before they were born. They are a part of their heritage. God created us to be tightly bonded with family.

*Help them live in the now.* When someone dies, our children often feel guilty for having fun and laughing. We need to assure them that the deceased would want us to enjoy life and it is not disrespectful.

We never know what's going on inside the heads and hearts of our children. We can only love them enough to allow them to own their feelings and express their fears. In the end they alone must come to terms with life—and with death.

----

*I remember going with my mother once to visit Justin's grave. We had bought a toy to leave for him at his headstone. I was quite young; I'm not sure of my age. But I do remember expecting God to come get the toy for my brother and take it to him before we left. I didn't want to leave until God came and got it for him. I don't quite remember how my mom eventually got me back into the car when it came time to go, but I was quite adamant about not leaving until God came and got my brother's toy for him. After all, I had brought it for him.*

*As I grew up, I was told that our bodies are buried and our spirits move on to heaven, where there is no more grief, illness, or pain. I came to realize that one day, through faith in Christ, I would be going to heaven to be with Justin. Even though visiting his gravesite brings me comfort, I know that a tombstone isn't the end.*

*Chapter 15*

# What Is Heaven Like?

*The scene is forever etched in my memory, somewhere midway between laughter and tears. Tiny three-year-old Jeff in tiny size-three swim trunks is standing over the dead carcass of a bee. I have just tried to dry his tears with the standard talk about bee stings: "See, honey, the bee got hurt worse than you did. He died for stinging you."*

*His response, finger pointed and with all the body language that accompanies a well-deserved scolding: "Don't you go to heaven and sting my brother, you naughty bee!"*

## What Do Children Say?

Children have a lot to teach us about heaven.

When his grandpa died, three-year-old Jason was concerned that Grandpa was roaming around heaven, bumping into clouds, and not able to find his way out. He had heard that they lost Grandpa and that he was in heaven.

Breanne, age four, says, "Heaven is a place where there are many, many, many, many angels, up in the sky. Jesus, God, and many, many angels and many other angels live there. Eve lives there, and my great-great grandma."

Kyle, age eleven, says, "Heaven is really, really, really, really beautiful and fun. We worship God all day but we still have fun. Nothing bad is going to be there, like Satan and tears and crying." It's important for an eleven-year-old boy to know that heaven will be fun!

Comedian Art Linkletter tells of a boy on his former television show, *Kids Say the Darndest Things.* The little boy seemed sad, so Art asked him if something was wrong. He said his dog had just died. Trying to comfort the little boy, Art told him that when he got to heaven, his dog would be there. The boy replied, "But what would God want with a dead dog?"[11]

*The worst thing we could do to our children would be to lie to them, to try to tell them we believe something we really don't.*

Children are the center of their universe. They don't realize anything happens while they are sleeping. They are concerned with the necessities of life: eating, sleeping, playing, and being comforted.

When the concept of heaven is introduced, they want to know who is taking care of their brother; who is clothing and feeding their sister; who their grandma is reading to or holding on her lap. We have a great opportunity to give them a glimpse of a world without pain, a world they too will inherit if they have faith in Jesus.

In some ways it is easier now to explain the concept of heaven than it was when Jeff was growing up. Angels and stories of God's providence are popular in today's culture. We even see them on television, almost daily. But children are very concrete and literal in their thinking.

We do so want to believe in the spectacular and supernatural. We want to believe good always wins. But life's contradictions face us with questions we can't answer. We need to provide our children with the best answers we have. When we give them pat or standard answers ("The good die young," "God needed Grandpa to help him," etc.), this is usually our attempt to assuage their grief by telling them half-truths, our attempt to have them believe something we're not really sure we believe ourselves. We must tell them the truth about life as we understand it. We should allow them to verbalize their questions without trying to protect them.

After we have shared our beliefs with our children, we must learn to say, "I don't know." The worst thing we could do to our children would be to lie to them, to try to tell them we believe something we really don't. We can say, "I don't understand it, but I believe . . ." or "I'm not sure about it, but I think . . ." or "It doesn't seem like it now, but I know God is good."

## What Does the Bible Say?

Partly because of our new fascination with angels, people today accept almost anything as true. Yet it is difficult to merge our Hollywood vision of God and his guardian angels, who are always watching over us and doing the miraculous because God loves us, with the reality that life doesn't always go as planned. It is hard for us to decipher what is God's truth and what is man's invention. We need to go to the source: the Bible.

*Jesus says he is preparing a place for us and will come again to get us to live with him (John 14:2–3).* Children understand a house being ready to move into. They understand a friend they love coming to their house to take them somewhere without their parents. We told Jeff that Jesus had Justin's house in heaven ready for him. When Justin's body was too sick for him to live in any longer, Jesus came to take him to heaven. He is now with Gammy and others who love him, too. The body he used to live in is here because he doesn't need this house anymore.

*Jesus said, "I am the way and the truth and the life. No one comes to the Father except through me" (John 14:6).* We need to tell our children that the way to heaven is through Jesus. When we ask Jesus to live in our hearts, he will come get us when we die, too. Heaven is a beautiful place. We may be afraid of being sick but we need not be afraid of dying.

*Jesus said God will dwell with us in heaven. There will be no more death, mourning, crying, or pain (Revelation 21:1–4).* We must assure our children that the one they love doesn't hurt anymore. Uncle Jim isn't sick anymore. We miss him but we are glad that he is now okay.

*The Bible teaches us that heaven is a beautiful city with great jewels and streets of gold (Revelation 21:19–21).* The things we work so hard for here will be given to us there. We are what is really important to God. Grandma is God's great treasure in heaven now. She has everything she needs.

*Nothing bad will ever enter heaven (Revelation 21:27).* Especially if the death was violent or tragic, our children worry about those they love being unprotected. We need to tell them, "Auntie May is safe there. No one can ever hurt her again."

*The Bible says that all animals will be tame there (Isaiah 11:6–9).* Although we know animals don't have souls, it is distressing to children to envision heaven without their favorite pet. Tell them, "We will be able to pet the wolf and play with the lions."

There are also things the Bible *doesn't* tell us about heaven. We don't know if those we love will grow older or will be the age they were when they died. We don't really know what we will do, except that it will be wonderful. So let your children imagine what it will be like.

The story is told of a little boy drawing a picture of God. His mother responded, "But no one has seen God. We don't know what he looks like."

The child's response was, "They will when I get through."

———————

*The comment I made is so true to what a three-year-old thinks of heaven: everyone and everything goes there. I didn't want that bee to sting my brother. I didn't want Justin to get hurt and cry like I had. I seemed to think it was my job to protect my little brother from the bad things in life.*

*As a child, I didn't know quite what to expect of heaven. I just knew it was where my brother and Gammy were and that one day I'd be able to go there to be with them. As I grew up, I thought it was this really bright place, because some grown-ups had told me that the streets were paved with gold and that it was really shiny there. I thought it would be a good idea to have sunglasses when I finally got to go.*

*Today I think of heaven as a golfing music fest. My family are singers and golfers, so I have been around both golf and music my whole life. In golf you never know whom you might be paired up with. You always meet somebody new or get to know somebody better. It's a nice time to visit if you go with your friends.*

*In terms of music, people seem to become closer to one another when they get to sing. For me it's just another excuse to hang out and enjoy each other's company. That is how I see heaven. It will be a wonderful reunion of long-lost friends who just visit and enjoy each other. We'll hang out, sing, enjoy each other's company . . . and of course play golf all the time.*

## Chapter 16

# What Is Forever?

*When will Justin come home, Mom?"*

*"Honey, Justin is in heaven. He can never come home. We can go to him someday, but he can never come back."*

*"But I want him to come back."*

*"I know, honey. I miss him, too."*

*"But when will he come home?"*

*"He can never come home. He died."*

*"Oh."*

---

I can't begin to tell you how many times Jeff and I had this conversation. Sometimes we had it several times a day. Sometimes we had it several times an hour. Sometimes—no, often—it left me in tears. As long as Jeff was asking the questions, I had to be saying the words: "He died. He can't come back." As painful as the process was, it helped me believe that it was indeed true. Our baby was dead.

Shock and denial is the first stage of grief. It is a physiological response. When we are frightened or stunned with the news of death, blood rushes from our extremities to our brain to give us the superhuman energy we need to go into fight-or-flight response. If we felt the full impact of the reality of death all at once, our bodies couldn't take it. We would die, too. God has graciously gifted us with this intuitive painkiller.

In today's world the process of dying usually happens in a hospital or rest home. We don't have to listen to our loved ones' cries or watch their pain when medication wears off. We don't have to change their diapers and wipe their fevered brows. This removes us from the reality of their death and delays our feeling the pain of loss. Emotional illnesses develop, however, if we fail to face the reality of our loss over time. We may try to get on with life and forget. Jeff's questions kept me from avoiding the truth and burying my grief. I had to answer him, so I had to hear myself say the words. It slowly became my truth, too. I couldn't run from the fact that I was the mother of the deceased. Wow! Those words still hurt.

But to our children, especially our young children, these questions and comments are words of curiosity. They have entered a world of mourning and a world of forever before they can comprehend the concept. To them this is the grief equivalent of a well-known conversation:

"How much longer till we get there?"

"Two minutes less than last time you asked."

## What Signs and Questions Show Us That Children Don't Understand?

Angela was just four when her father died. She could not understand that death was final; he was just away and would come back later. Over a year after he died, her mother bought a new car. When she brought it home to show the girls, Angela said,

"Won't Daddy be surprised to see our car!" Again her mother had the painful task of telling her children that Daddy would not be coming home.

Eva Marie was ten when her grandfather died. She remembers being extremely angry with the person who told her he died, and not believing it. The memory of her mother collapsing as they closed his casket haunted her. Four years later when her first boyfriend was killed in a hunting accident, she knew that death was final, and the depth of her mother's pain was inside her.

Children show us they don't understand when they

- talk as though the deceased were still alive.
- ask direct questions that reveal their confusion.
- show anger toward another person who reminds them of their loved one (a "new grandma," for example).
- include an imaginary friend when they play with toys, dolls, and friends.
- draw pictures that portray the deceased as though he or she was still alive.

We don't comprehend forever, either. When one we love dies, we understand it intellectually, but it may take us years to believe it inside. We think we see them when we walk into a restaurant. We pass another car and do a double-take because the person who died appears to be driving it. We plan our day to include a visit with a loved one, before we remember he or she is not here anymore. Short of death, when we have a life problem, we face it, fix it, and move on. When death happens, we can't fix it and move on. It is forever; it is nonnegotiable. Eternity is difficult to comprehend, no matter what our age.

## How Can We Help Our Children Understand?

Since animals are often a child's first experience with death, they provide us with a wealth of teaching opportunities and illustrations.

*Help them say good-bye.* Dr. Sandra Herron, director of both the singles ministry and the Fuqua School of Christian Communication at the Crystal Cathedral, shares a touching story about when her grandson Ian said good-bye to their Dalmatian, Lacy: "Ian arrived with tears in his giant velvet-brown eyes to say good-bye. Being only five years old, he had not mastered all the sounds of the English language yet, so his farewell message had a particularly poignant tone. As he patted her gently, he said, 'Well, Wacy, I guess this is it. You have been a good dog. You have been a vewy good dog. We did wots of fun things together. I wuv you and I'm weawy going to miss you. I'm going to miss you a wot. But don't wowwy, Wacy, don't be scared; evewy things is going to be awight, and someday we will see each other again. You know, in heaven. So good-bye, Wacy, good-bye. I wuve you.'"

*Understand that death triggers related losses.* The Norwoods adopted an orphan from China, now their precious six-year-old, Sarah Zheng-Kang. She continues to work through abandonment issues. The death of their dog, Cotton-Candi, brought many issues of loss to the surface. In Marcia's words, "I have not always been the teacher. I have learned from the way Sarah ZK has coped with these losses. Sarah speaks as if heaven is another country, far away, in the same way she talks about her homeland, China. She even looked for heaven on our world map."

Heart wrenching as these experiences are, these children will have a much easier time understanding death because they experienced it with loving parents to guide them through.

It is normal for children to repeat the same question. Young children are experiencing natural curiosity or confusion. The hurt you feel when these questions are repeated is your grief; for children, forever is somewhere between ten minutes and two hours.

Over and over children will ask, "But *when* will she be back?" Over and over we must say, "She will never be back here, but we can go to her someday."

----

*I have always been fascinated by death. Watching how different people go through the process of a funeral has always intrigued me. Some go to viewings and others don't. Some people cry a lot at the services, and others wait until they are alone. There seems to be a lot of ways to pay your final respects to those who have died.*

*One thing I have observed is that people, regardless of their style, always need closure. Funerals can provide us with this. Whether or not your children attend the service, it's very important that you help them find some sort of closure.*

*I remember for a long time wanting Justin to come back. There had been so much talk of me getting a little brother to play with, and I had always wanted to have one. Missing him was hard, since we couldn't go to heaven on vacation to visit. I still wonder at times what it would have been like to have a sibling around. I wonder how different my life would have been had Justin lived.*

# Part 4

## Tough Questions Children Don't Ask

$S$hortly after Justin came home, we planned a much needed vacation. When we got the call that my grandfather was dying, we changed our vacation to a trip to Garden Grove, California, to visit our extended family so we would have a chance to say good-bye.

It had been a bittersweet time together. On Memorial Day we settled in to enjoy the annual Strawberry Festival Parade. Alton and Margie live in a cul-de-sac on the parade route. We were warned that only in the case of an emergency would anyone be allowed out the day of the parade, so if we wanted to leave, we should park around the corner. We were so exhausted from the many days in the hospital with Justin and the many visits to the hospital to see my grandfather that we gladly kept our cars blocked in for an excuse to relax and enjoy the day.

Jeff awoke that morning, eager to see the parade, and walked into our room. We took one look at him and panicked—his left eye was crossed. We were five hours away from our pediatrician, whom we called away from his festivities. He first suggested that we come home immediately. Finally he agreed to let us take Jeff to a local emergency room. Almost as an afterthought I asked, "What do you think it might be? What would you do if he were your child?"

*His response left no doubt that what we were facing was urgent and potentially serious.*

*My sister-in-law quickly called her neurosurgeon, who offered to meet us in his office. We were escorted by the police through the parade route. The neurosurgeon examined Jeff thoroughly but was unable to find anything wrong. He told us to enjoy the weekend and have more tests run when we returned home.*

*We discovered in ensuing years that Jeff has a vision disorder which intensifies under stress. He struggled with it throughout his school career. If he was extremely nervous over a test, he would do poorly on it because his eye slightly crossed and he couldn't see some of the words.*

*The week after Justin died, Jeff's eye crossed again even though he was wearing his glasses. The doctor told us not to even mention it to him but to envelop him in love. Wise doctor!*

*Years later during another Strawberry Festival Parade, I told Jeff the story of the time he got a police escort out of Grandpa's house. He asked, "Did they believe you that it was an emergency?"*

*My honest answer: "They took one look at me and didn't even ask."*

---

If the only problems associated with death involved questions children ask, we could answer them. We could even anticipate them. This book would have been much easier to write. The difficult issues are the questions and concerns that become apparent in our children's bodies or in their behavior. Our task is to anticipate their unspoken and probably unconscious questions. Sometimes the questions are intentionally buried because our children don't know how to express their emotions or don't want to cause us more pain. Sometimes children are consciously unaware of these issues, but they manifest themselves in mysterious fevers, fears, and behavior changes.

The signs of grief may be outward and immediate, or there may be no signs until adulthood. Withdrawal from play, regression in potty training, changes in personality or behavior, and nightmares are common symptoms of grief in young children. A drop in school performance, withdrawal from social interaction, retreat into fantasy, rebellion (beyond what is normal for the age), and substance abuse sometimes occur among older children and teens after a death in a family. These reactions are a reflection of anger, guilt, fear, and confusion. If not dealt with in the years that immediately follow the death, a child's unshed tears and stifled questions swell and fester until adulthood. There they appear as extreme perfectionism, obsessive or destructive behaviors (eating disorders, addictions to drugs or alcohol, dependencies on other people, etc.), or the inability to form intimate relationships.

We parents need to anticipate our children's questions, model for them healthy expressions of emotion, and provide an environment in which these expressions are both safe and normal. This isn't as easy as it seems.

In Deuteronomy 33:25 God promises, "Your strength will equal your days." Before our terrible year I thought that verse meant that Christians wouldn't face severe tragedies. Now I realize that it really means that *when* we Christians face unbearable and difficult times, God will walk with us. Jeff's crossed eye, although traumatic, was one of those instances in which we were blessed by God in the midst of our tragedy. The Lord reminded us that he had hand-selected our medical professionals. My sister-in-law had been telling us that her doctor was the best in the nation and that we should bring Justin to him for care, even if we had to relocate to do it. She was concerned about Jeff but delighted to have a chance to get us in to see her neurosurgeon. She had already discussed Justin's condition at length with him.

After he finished with Jeff that day, he examined Justin. He asked, "Who is your neurosurgeon?" When we responded, "Dr. Bonner," his eyes lit up. He said, "Oh, he trained me. You're in wonderful hands."

---

*One of my elementary school friends lived with her single mother and visited her dad on weekends. Her mom became engaged. My friend was quite happy for her mother, but there was a question troubling her. Would her mother's marriage mean she wouldn't get to see her dad anymore? She wanted to ask her mom but was afraid because she thought it might make her mother and soon-to-be stepdad mad at her.*

*To adults the answer is so simple and obvious. To a child the question was overwhelming—so overwhelming that she didn't get up the courage to ask. Her question went unspoken because she feared for her well-being. Many of my questions went unasked because I feared they would further hurt my mother. I'm sure my friend's mother, father, and soon-to-be stepfather would have loved to ease her concern and help her open up. They just didn't know she was worried.*

*I still sometimes live in a fantasy world and sometimes want God to be a superhero. This past year I have struggled a lot with the truth behind Deuteronomy 33:25. I went through a difficult job change and relocation. The dreamer part of me wanted to see a grand miracle that would enable me to move up professionally without having to move geographically. Looking back with twenty-twenty hindsight, I realize now that the promise of God is not always a grand miracle but enough strength to get through my days. I made it through the last year of my life—barely. Just as God gave us strength for our daily needs during the tragedy of my brother's death, he does for me each day.*

*When talking with children, it is important to be careful of your reactions to what they say. A simple look can determine how open they will be. Things they say will not be easy to hear at times, but it's important to willingly listen to what your children have to say.*

## Chapter 17

# Did I Cause It?

*Jeff* called a buddy he hadn't seen in a few months to discuss their high school graduation plans. He was surprised to learn that his friend might not graduate. Now, helping at-risk students is what I do professionally. The fact that one of Jeff's buddies might not graduate came as a challenge to me. I felt badly that although I didn't work directly with his school, I had let a friend slip through the cracks. I should have asked much sooner. I called his mother.

I learned that Johnson had not done anything since he returned to school after Christmas vacation. He had been sitting and staring into space most of the time. He was failing at least one required course and doing poorly in all of his classes. His teacher told his mother she noticed the change immediately after vacation. The teacher suspected drugs but didn't know what to do about it, so she did nothing—until failure notices came out five months later and she notified his family that he probably would not graduate.

I asked his mother what had happened over Christmas vacation. Her mother—Johnson's grandmother and his best friend and, in his eyes, the only person in all the world who loved him unconditionally—had died. How sad that a teacher noticed but did nothing! How sad that a teacher suspected drugs but didn't intervene! How sad that a child sat alone in his grief! How sad that a normal grief reaction so drastically changed a child's future.

Johnson hadn't been a perfect child. Part of the grief he bore was his own guilt. Oh yes, every grandma alive knows that all little boys and girls are

*sometimes naughty, and they love them anyway. But a bereaved little boy—
and, as in this case, a bereaved big boy—must work through guilt. In that
process Johnson struggled with the possibility that in some way he had con-
tributed to his grandmother's death.*

---

Children view the world with themselves at its center, and
guilt almost always accompanies an unwanted change in their circumstances. Children struggling with guilt will become extreme
in their behavior. They may become perfectionistic and less play-
ful. They may become naughty or clingy. Some of these traits are
normal for their personality. Carried to excess, or if they represent a change in behavior, they are a reaction to grief.

We need to speak the truth in words over and over again:

"Grandpa died because he was sick [or in an accident]."
"It was not your fault [or 'You are forgiven']."
"You did nothing wrong [or 'What you did was wrong,
but you have asked God to forgive you. We all make
mistakes. Let's learn from this together']."

## How Do Children Express Deep Emotion?

Myrna was eight when her grandfather died following a
stroke. The day he died, she had been making mud pies for him
and left the hose stretched across the yard. While she was away,
he fell. As she stood by his side rubbing his hand and arm, they
became colder and colder, and he slipped into eternity. She
believed for years that she killed him, both from hearing comments that he tripped on the hose and from not understanding
that her rubbing his arm had nothing to do with his death, except

perhaps to make it more pleasant. She says she probably went into nursing as penance for killing her favorite grandfather. Ten years later, in nurse's training, she learned she wasn't guilty. Once she resolved the issue of guilt, her nursing career ended.

*In children guilt is often expressed as anger.*

When death comes to the family, a child may think he or she caused it. Self-esteem can be shattered if these guilty feelings are not addressed. In children guilt is often expressed as anger. Children may say terrible things about one who died. They may be angry when you try to talk about it. This too is normal. If you punish them for these emotions, their feelings are buried. Rather than punishing them (unless it is for the chosen words, etc.), help them to express what they feel and to learn tools to manage their emotions.

When children don't learn healthy ways to express their anger, they either act out or build a wall around themselves. We have many teens today who are self-medicating by using drugs and alcohol because they never learned a healthy way to express anger. The end result of anger turned inward is sometimes suicide. Sadly, in America suicide is the number three cause of death for people fifteen to twenty-four years old, and the sixth leading cause of death for people five to fourteen years of age.[12] We *must* help our children make friends with their emotions.

In studies on anger, children who were taught to hit a punching bag when they were angry were actually angrier *after* the experience than before. However, it has been my experience that those who can verbalize their feelings and anger to God while they hit the punching bag experience relief. More than that, they let God become their partner in grieving.

## How Can We Help Our Children Deal with Guilt?

When our children express their guilt to us, we intuitively try to talk them out of it:

"Honey, you didn't cause that."
"You didn't mean to."
"But you were hurting."
"Oh, Grandpa has forgiven you."

These may all be true, but they have a big problem attached: we don't have the power to forgive sin. Whether it is legitimate guilt or not, the *first* place our children should go with their confession is to God: "If we confess our sins, he is faithful and just and will forgive us our sins and purify us from all unrighteousness" (I John 1:9). It is simply too good to be true! God has become the atoning sacrifice for our sins. When we take them to him, we are purified. What a great gift to give our children:

"I know you're sorry, honey, and I know you didn't mean to,
    but let's ask Jesus to forgive you."
"You didn't cause Grandpa to die, but if you feel guilty
    about it, let's talk to Jesus."

When we rationalize and make excuses for our children, we actually short-circuit their relationship with God and dull their conscience. The only antidote to guilt is God's forgiveness. Let's encourage them instead to ask forgiveness from God and from the person who needs to forgive them. Only then can we truly help them forgive themselves and gain perspective. What a great opportunity to teach a valuable life skill!

*I remember when my grandmother was in the hospital dying from cancer. She was in an intensive care unit. I had gone in to visit her. It was just the two of us. Apparently nobody had told her yet how serious the cancer was, but I didn't know that. She asked me what the doctors said. She demanded that I tell her the truth. So I very bluntly said that it didn't look good. After that I was told it was a bad move to let her know what was going on. In my mind I was just being honest with my grandmother.*

*A day or two later at a summer school class I was taking, someone who knew the family asked me how she was doing, and I didn't answer because I didn't want to be scolded later. That response was out of guilt.*

As an adult, I can now tell the difference between unnecessary guilt and real guilt. I have a group of friends who hold me accountable to them and to God. They help me think through what I'm dealing with, so my confession of sins to God is motivated by legitimate guilt rather than self-imposed or parent-imposed or society-imposed shame.

When the kids I work with are being disciplined for inappropriate behaviors, they usually start acting worse. In a way they are saying, "You thought I was bad then; I'm really going to be bad now." This is a guilt reaction from kids who were never taught about the freedom of confession to God or about accountability for their actions.

For example, one day a child at the school where I work was reprimanded for interrupting another student who was trying to ask a question. He continued interrupting and yelling until I had to remove him from class to help him calm down. After we talked, he was able to return to class and apologized to his teacher and those he had offended.

As parents, it is your job to help your children recognize God's voice and confess their sins. It is also your job to help them know from their hearts that they are cleansed from all unrighteousness when God hears them. In addition, they need to learn about accountability. The resolution of guilt isn't just saying, "I was wrong." It is admitting it, learning from it, and learning how to do things differently the next time you are in a similar situation.

## Chapter 18

# If I Get Sick, Will I Die, Too?

*O*h, *the agony of the nightmares! I discovered that Jeff's nightmares, like grief, would come in waves. Something would trigger them, I know not what, and they would return, unannounced and uninvited. They would last from a few nights to a few weeks. Then they would disappear as suddenly as they came.*

*When we went through what I now refer to as a season of nightmares and fears, Jeff would usually sleep with me. Then as peaceful sleep returned, I would urge him back into his bed. For a few nights I would stay with him until he fell asleep; then for a few nights I would put him to bed amid protests, assuring him I was right next door.*

*Jeff is normally asleep by the time his head hits the pillow, but during these nightmare seasons he had trouble falling asleep. Every few minutes he would call me. I would hold him and ask him what was wrong. He would say he was afraid to be alone. I would explain to him that he was never alone, because Jesus was always there.*

*One night after one of my great theological dissertations, I returned to my bed feeling smug and proud. A few minutes later I heard Jeff call:*

*"Mom, I'm getting kind of tired of lying here with Jesus. Can I come sleep with you?"*

"If I get sick, will I die, too?" is rarely a question that is verbalized. Rather it is expressed in fears. The fears are real. Sometimes they come out through nightmares, as in Jeff's case. Sometimes children will avoid sleep or will exhibit changes in their normal routines. They may cling to you, not wanting you out of their sight. They may think they have all the symptoms of the person who died:

"Mom, my leg aches, too. I think I have cancer."
"Dad, I have a headache. I have a brain tumor, too."
"Please pray for me, Miss Stuart. I have leukemia."

## What Behaviors Say Children Are Dealing with the Fear of Dying?

In general, any major change in a child's behavior might be attributed to grief:

Refusing to visit friends or leave parents
Normally gregarious but suddenly shy
Once rebellious and now submissive
A neatnik who is now messy
A potty-trained child who suddenly wets the bed

When these nightmares, fears, and changes in behavior occur, our children are having a normal emotional reaction to the death of one they love. What they are really saying is, "Will I die, too?" The world as they know it has been turned upside down. Right now nothing makes sense; what they trusted has disappeared. Their reactions tell you they don't understand, they don't like what has happened, and they want life to go back to the way it was before.

## What Can We Do to Help Our Children?

Since our children's reactions are emotional, we need to help them at an emotional level. We parents, you see, are great at intellectualizing. If we can do that, we don't have to feel our own pain as keenly.

If only kissing it would make it go away! Understand that their behavior is an expression of pain. Treat them as children you deeply love who have a broken heart. Don't allow them to get away with wrong behavior, but overlook the minor infractions.

*When nightmares, fears, and changes in behavior occur, our children are having a normal emotional reaction to the death of one they love. What they are really saying is, "Will I die, too?"*

At these times our children need us at their side. They need our touch; they need our love; they need us to listen to them and reassure them. They are faced with their own mortality much sooner than they should be, but they are too young to understand the truth.

Talk to them. Explain death to them as you understand it.

Listen to what they say, without censoring or correcting it.

Have them tell you what it means to die.

Help them realize that naughty behavior isn't okay, even when they're frustrated.

More importantly, hold them. Love them. Help them fall asleep. Read to them. Leave a light on if they need it. Leave a door open if it helps. Their ability to trust and to discern is being developed. In a world that has just dealt their family a mortal blow, they need to know they can count on you just to be there. If they can trust you, they will find it easier to trust God.

Now to another tough issue—the truth: "If I get sick, will I die, too?"

> "Everyone gets sick sometimes, and most of the time people get well. Remember when Grandma was in the hospital? We visited her and prayed for her, and now she's home."

> "Eventually everyone dies. When they do, they will go to heaven if they had faith in Jesus."

> "Someday, we hope not for a long, long time, you will die, too. When you do, your spirit will leave your body, and you will get a healthy new body in heaven. You will see your sister again when you get to heaven. In heaven you will never die or be sick again."

> "Every day you spend on earth is special. Your sister would want you to have fun and play and enjoy your friends. If she were here, she would tell you that."

---

*I don't remember having nightmares at all. The only thing I do remember is having a difficult time falling asleep one night because I was missing Justin. I think that's one night I ended up sleeping with my mom.*

*I spent a lot of time sleeping in her bed, although I just remember it being an excuse to be with my mom. I don't remember ever associating any other feelings with it, except that I didn't want to be in my room.*

*We had a dog at the first place I worked out of college. The kids all loved the dog but he was quite old. He was eventually put to sleep because he had severe arthritis. Having a dog put to sleep is traumatic for both children and adults. There were a couple of children who were afraid to go to sleep that night because they thought they might end up dead like the dog.*

*For a young child to be asking questions such as "If I get sick, will I die, too?" makes complete sense. It is a way for their young, concrete minds to internalize death.*

*Death needs to be presented as a normal part of life. Children need to be taught this from an early age, even though it is the hardest thing for adults to deal with, let alone teach a young child.*

---

The nightmares were so traumatic to me as I helped Jeff through them that I was sure he would carry them as scars all his life. He remembers missing Justin; he remembers sleeping with me. But he doesn't remember the trauma that brought it about.

I hope he doesn't remember the nightmares because I held him and loved him and prayed for him. I want to believe that I had something to do with it and that it was healthy. Then I remember the times I failed him and realize there must have been someone greater than me involved.

Lots of people have opinions about the traumatic things we don't remember:

- Psychologists might say Jeff's experience was so painful that it is a buried memory.
- Theologians might say that God was with Jeff, so he carries no scars.
- Sociologists might speculate that Jeff has worked through it.

Well, what does this mother say?

If it is a buried memory, I will stand by his side as he cries the tears yet to be uncovered. Buried memories rob us of energy for today. If he needs to go into his past in order to be free, we'll face it together. I want him to walk in truth, even when it means I have to face my own failures.

God was and is with my son, but he still bears scars. They are part of what gives him character. The scars don't discredit God. The fact that he is bigger than our scars and that he uses them for his good makes him awesome. I don't truly understand God or his ways, but I am so glad he loves me. Whatever Jeff faces, God too will be his partner.

If Jeff has worked through it, he remembers it with sadness. He may still cry tears, but they are tears of sorrow rather than tears of defeat. It is sad that his brother died. Life really isn't fair.

Now I understand that one you love doesn't ever really die, because he or she is always a part of you. I still glean from my loved ones, even those who have lived in heaven for many years.

I love you, Jeff. I will be with you as you negotiate your journey through life, whether in person (when you wish I would be silent) or through death (when you will wish I could talk).

## Chapter 19

# Will You Die and Leave Me, Too?

*The fear of abandonment. It's gripping! If I moved three feet from where we were and Jeff wasn't looking, he would go into a state of utter panic. He would run in every direction, looking for me. Then he would head for the parking lot, trying to find our car.*

*When he was just a toddler, I found him in the parking lot three times. He was glad to see me, and I was sobbing hysterically. I would hug him and ask him what happened. He thought I had left him. Over and over again I would say, "Jeff, I will never leave you. Never go outside again. Go to the nearest sales clerk and ask her to call me."*

*But it happened again and again. In a split second he would be gone. Finally he abandoned the parking lot but ran zigzag through the shopping center. He would be so distraught, he couldn't even remember my name and couldn't see me standing a few feet away.*

*We rehearsed it so many, many times:*

*"What will you do?"*

*"Go to the nearest sales clerk and ask her to find you."*

*"Good! I love you. I would never leave without you."*

*The last time this happened, he was nine years old. I was in line to pay for my purchase and decided to switch colors. Glancing at Jeff playing with a toy nearby, I walked a few feet to the clothes rack. When I got back in line less than one minute later, Jeff was gone.*

*I frantically asked the clerk to have him paged. She told me I had to go in person from the first to the third floor of the store to report a lost child.*

*Panicking, I looked in one direction to the parking lot, another to the escalator in the middle of the store. Torn over which to check first, I quickly glanced out the door before hurrying toward the escalator.*

*There he was, in the comforting arms of the clerk in the handbag section. After I hugged him, I turned to the clerk. "He panics and runs away. We've been working on this. Was he even able to talk with you? Could he tell you our names?"*

*She responded, "He didn't know his name; he didn't know your name, but he told me you were wearing white pants and carrying a shoulder bag. Then"—she chuckled—"he told me how old you are!"*

———

Regardless of their age, children may react to the loss of a loved one with what psychologists call separation anxiety. They may exhibit behaviors that are the result of the fear that they will lose another loved one. They often express this anxiety by refusing to spend the night at a grandparent's house; developing illnesses or refusing to go to bed when left with a baby-sitter; quietly sitting in a classroom but doing no work if a parent is out of town; attempting to sabotage friendships; stealing; lying; etc. All of these behaviors are a plea, in the only way the child knows how to bargain, for someone else not to die, too.

Fear of abandonment is what Dr. Schuller calls the ultimate hurt. He believes that when we conquer this one, we can conquer anything else life hands us.[13]

## How Is Fear of Abandonment Expressed in Children?

In younger children fear of abandonment may be verbalized, or it may be expressed in behavior, as in Jeff's case. The younger the child, the more likely they are to ask direct questions. Alyssa, age five, is concerned that her Grassie is getting old. She asks lots of questions about death and dying. One day, on the way to the store, she asked Grassie what happens when we die. Grassie told her we go to be with God. Alyssa responded, "He shouldn't make us die. He has enough up there already."

Fevers, illnesses, phobias, not wanting parents out of their sight—all these are signs of fear of abandonment. Sometimes this fear is even expressed as contentment. When I left Jeff for business trips happy, spoiled, cared for by grandparents, I often came home to a teacher conference because he sat all day staring into space, with a smile on his face, doing nothing. When his grandparents put him to bed, he would pray, "Dear God, please help my mommy to come home."

*We must not allow our children's sorrow to become an excuse for bad behavior; we must not blame everything naughty they do on their grief. But we cannot overlook their hurt and fear.*

As children grow, they will ask more questions. Periodically their behavior will show their concerns. We must not allow their sorrow to become an excuse for bad behavior; we must not blame everything naughty they do on their grief. But we cannot overlook their hurt and fear.

Perhaps recognizing our own fears and behavior changes brought on by our loss will help us recognize and empathize with this fear in our children. Do you sometimes check on your children in the middle of the night to make sure they're still breathing? Do you worry about them if they sleep too late in the morning? Do you stay awake and pray an extra prayer when they'll be out late with friends? Do you wonder what would happen to them if something terrible happened to you?

I do. When death has visited too soon and too close, we never again take life for granted. I wish I could get over it, but it's not all that bad. I pray more now. I listen better. Yes, I know all this is symbolic of a lack of faith, because God is in control. And yes, I love God and say I trust him to work everything out for my good. But he doesn't always do things the way I tell him, so I have to face the fact that I don't really trust him as I should. That drives me to know him better. That's a good thing.

## What Can We Do to Assure Our Children?

*Teach it before they need it.* Dan was sixteen when he found a special friend. He trusted Charla and for the first time talked from his heart. She also shared intimately with him. He left with that special afterglow that comes when you first are vulnerable and someone understands, when someone accepts you just as you are. The next night Charla fell asleep at the steering wheel and entered eternity. That day Dan says he lost his innocence about life and death in addition to losing a dear friend. No one had ever talked with him about death. He believes a loving introduction to death could have at least cushioned his pain.

Our young children need to be told of death in natural, normal, assuring ways. If they don't learn about death in a healthy way when they are young, it is especially traumatic when they hit their teen years. Dan's first encounter with the concept of death shouldn't have been at age sixteen. But his story is symbolic of millions who have been protected by parents who genuinely want to spare their children emotional pain. Children can handle it much easier than adults if they are talked with, listened to, and loved through it.

*Build in traditions and rituals.* Jeff's abandonment issues were deep, and my job involved travel. I felt guilty every time I left him. I sought another job and counseling. The job never materialized, but the counselor taught me to deal with his abandonment fear by calling daily at a set time. That eased his anxiety. He also helped me understand that in addition to having a legitimate fear of abandonment, Jeff had learned to press my guilt button. Knowing that eased my anxiety and empowered me as a parent.

*Let them know you worry, too.* As Jeff grew older and began going out with friends, we created a new ritual: the phone call home. With that came a slogan: It's okay to be late; it's okay to change your mind. It's never okay to worry your mother!

*Tell the truth.* Our children need to be told the truth, in love. We can't promise, "I won't die." We don't hold life and death in our hands. We can promise, "I will always love you," "I would never leave you at the store," "I plan to come back on Friday. If something terrible should happen to me, Grandma will take care of you. And remember to trust in Jesus so we'll meet again."

---

*I remember that incident in the store. I'm not sure what ran through my head during those times, but I know I was scared. I had just dealt with Dad leaving, Justin dying, Gammy dying, Daboy dying, and Wally dying, all in a short amount of time. If all those people left, then why wouldn't my mom leave, too?*

*I have seen similar behavior in the children I work with. One of the first kids I worked with was placed in residential treatment because of violent behaviors and other problems. His mom was diabetic. A few weeks before he was placed in treatment, his mom had a diabetic attack. He was the only one home and was responsible for his mom getting the help she needed. He literally saved her life.*

*While he was with us, he always wanted to call his mother or go home for weekends, just to make sure she was doing well. He asked repeatedly, "But what if something happens, and I'm not there to help her again?" He had this deep fear that she would die and they would never see each other again.*

*In another case, a child was having quite a time behaviorally. We finally got him on track and he was doing well. This good behavior lasted for two months before he got into a bit of trouble over a minor problem. It wasn't that big a deal, but when we started to discipline him for it, his personality dramatically changed. He thought he was going to get the worst consequence we could give him, and he ran away. This made things worse than they should have been. After we caught him and brought him back, he told his therapist that he thought he was going to be kicked out and sent back to juvenile hall. We comforted him and reminded him that juvenile hall was for serious assaultive issues, not for some minor infraction. It is difficult for these troubled children to discern the seriousness of their crime.*

*Given the children I work with, I'm concerned about parental discipline. When children who are afraid of being abandoned are emotional, they need to be loved, held, encouraged to talk, and assured of your commitment to them. When they have recovered from their emotional reactions, we need to talk to them and help them learn to use good judgment. My mom went to the extreme in terms of nurturing. The parents of the children I work with go to the extreme in terms of punishment. We need to have a balance of both in our lives.*

## Chapter 20

# If I Talk About It,
# Will It Make You Sad?

*Life was so traumatic then. Every little change, every little decision, was heavy.*

*I decided to teach a night class; I needed the money, and I needed a break from the house that constantly reminded me of my sorrow. My class consisted of thirty business owners in search of skills for writing effective letters.*

*The first evening was uneventful on the home front. When I got ready to leave for the second class session, however, Jeff began clinging to me and begging me not to go. I hugged him to assure him he would be okay with his favorite baby-sitter. That's when I felt his forehead—hot!*

*I knew he wasn't seriously ill, but I didn't want to leave him with a fever. I realized too that thirty business owners had already left their places of business and would be awaiting my arrival. I decided to go for the first half of class, call to check on Jeff, and dismiss class at break if he needed me.*

*When I called an hour and a half later, his temperature was normal and he was sound asleep. He slept uneventfully through the night and awoke the next morning as though nothing had happened.*

---

Actually, it hurt my feelings: Jeff would talk about Justin to family and friends but not to me. They would tell me touching or funny things he said, but when I tried to talk with him, he acted as though I were prying where I didn't belong. Occasionally I would read his thoughts and feelings about Justin in his schoolwork.

One day I brought up the subject, asking him why he didn't talk with me. I discovered he hated to talk to me because it made me cry, which hurt him more. I did two things: I reassured him that it's okay for mothers to cry and that tears are healthy, and I thanked God for friends who would listen.

## Why Do Some Children Talk, While Others Are Silent?

Children come in all flavors, shapes, and sizes. Some will readily talk. When we listen to them, our hearts ache and we worry that they are forever broken because of life's circumstances. Usually once they have talked, these children are able to let their grief go. The process of talking frees them.

Other children appear not to be affected by death because they are of a temperament that keeps busy to deal with grief. They may bury themselves in their schoolwork or in their involvement with their organization of choice. Part of their constructive energy is in loving memory of the one who died. Busyness is their grief work.

Other children are intuitively listeners. They watch as everything happens around them, but they don't talk. They don't know enough to talk yet. They have watched us reduced to tears, and they don't want to cause us to cry anymore. They are prone to processing their grief through listening, thinking, and occasionally talking with a friend. They may enjoy journaling or writing as an outlet.

Still other children process grief from deep within. They are often our musicians and artists. They will write touching letters, essays, and songs. They may draw pictures that paint a thousand words. They are using their talents to process their grief.

> *Grief is painful work. Grief involves tears. Grief festers if not dealt with.*

All of these are healthy reactions. Grief is painful work. Grief involves tears. Grief festers if not dealt with.

Unresolved and unacknowledged grief expresses itself in fevers, illnesses, phantom pains, and phobias. Jeff was moving into a realm of unhealthy grief in the opening story. Had I made fun of him or ignored his needs, had I told only the baby-sitter that I would call, it could have had lasting consequences. Instead I sat Jeff down and told him where I was going. I told him what time I would call. I told him how long it would take me to get home if he became worse or needed me. We became partners in the process of grieving. Once his need for reassurance was met, his anxiety-induced fever subsided.

## How Do We Balance Children's Needs with Ours?

When are we being selfish? When are we being melodramatic? When should we talk with children even if they don't want to talk? When should we allow them time alone? When should we invite over a wise and listening friend? When should we handle this one ourselves? When should we go to fulfill our obligations? When should we stay home in spite of prior commitments because our children need us?

Answer these questions and you can become rich overnight! We all want to know. Parenting is a series of on-the-job decisions. Sometimes we make the right ones. Sometimes they are harmful.

Much of the time any of several options are healthy. Most of the time we don't really know if we made the right choice.

There are, however, some life principles that might help.

*Go with your instinct most of the time.* We train ourselves to use our head rather than our heart. In matters of parenting, usually our heart is right.

*Never stifle an honest expression of grief.* Grief comes in waves, in us and in our children. When these waves hit us, talk, cry, welcome the tears. If we don't express our tears when they come, they will go inside and hurt us. No, we don't want to grieve forever, uncontrollably. We also don't want to teach our children that tears are only for the weak.

*Do whatever's next.* Hazel Lee, mother of Iranian hostage Gary Lee, said she was preparing to teach a Sunday school lesson when she got the call informing her of Gary's capture. She fell to her knees sobbing. Then she asked, "God, what do I do?" He replied, "Whatever's next." She taught her Sunday school class.[14]

*Look for a sense of peace.* Usually a deep sense of peace accompanies the best decisions; a deep sense of confusion or uneasiness accompanies the poorer ones.

*Make sure your children know you are on their team.* So often in the aftermath of grief, we find ourselves yelling at our children rather than explaining and listening to them. When that happens, we need a time-out. Then we need a time together to listen, cry, pray, and recommit ourselves to being a family.

*Remember laughter.* Laughter and tears are actually twins. Nothing cleanses the soul like a good heart cry. Nothing clears the cobwebs and binds us like a good belly laugh.

*Several times I remember talking to my mom about things that were tough. As a young boy of about nine or ten, I remember her subtle reactions. She would get these looks of anguish on her face. She tried to hide them, but I would see these looks, especially when I shared a little of how I felt about Dad and how he treated me. It seemed as if my struggles made our already hard times worse. She tried getting me to talk about my brother's death and my dad not being around, but I felt I was causing her more pain.*

*I still don't like talking to my mom about life's pain. Her reaction (out of her heart of love) to my already hard times makes it harder on me. If the pain in my life causes those around me to hurt, then I feel as though I have made things worse. I think that's why I still today find myself talking to those who aren't as close to the situation causing me grief, rather than telling someone who will end up in tears because of the grief I'm struggling with. They seem to have this degree of separation that allows them to listen to me empathetically.*

*Mom tells me that sharing in heartaches is a mother's job and, hurt or not, she's there for me. She also tells me that talking with parents who care makes it easier for us to trust God with our struggles. I'm not a parent yet but I think that's good advice. I also think parents should make sure their children have many other healthy adults in their lives, because children need lots of mentors.*

*Although I don't like asking for help, I am blessed to have people who care about me enough to help when I get around to asking for it—even the people who are emotionally involved, like my mom.*

*Chapter 21*

# If I'm Naughty, Will You Die?

*The first time Jeff forged my signature, he was in kindergarten. On the bottom of his homework paper that I was supposed to read and sign, he printed the words "Jeff's mom."*

*The conference that followed was not the first conversation I'd had with Mrs. Patterson. By the time Jeff had been in kindergarten five weeks, I had been invited to four parent conferences to discuss his behavior. Jeff would stare into space but do nothing. In one conference she kept referring to him as bright. I commented, "I've never really cared if he is bright. I want him to be happy."*

*She responded, "I don't know what he knew when he got here."*

*I told her that he knew his alphabet but none of his letter sounds. I had tried to teach him but he didn't want to learn. I figured he wasn't ready.*

*She replied, "Then your son isn't bright; he's brilliant. He has ignored every word I've said, and he knows them all now."*

*It is always a mystery to me how stupid dishonesty is. Jeff was certainly not in trouble. There was no logical reason why he should hide the paper from me.*

*As we talked about it, I asked, "Jeff, why didn't you let me see that paper?"*

*He said, "I didn't want to bother you."*

*As I learn more about grief, I realize there was a big and troublesome message behind that action. In his young mind he had reasoned it out. He had to be really good and not cause me any trouble so I wouldn't die and leave him, too.*

Trying to be very good is a common childhood reaction to grief. Mary remembers her mother going to the hospital to deliver her brother Mark. Mark lived only fifteen minutes and died of respiratory failure. Mary's father instructed the children to take care of their mother. When she came home, they all sat silently as close to her as they could get, but no one talked. Her Mom told her about her angel brother in heaven. Now, over forty years later, she remembers him that way and thinks of her silence as a gift to her mother, who came home from the hospital with empty arms.

Dorothy didn't have to be told that Grandpa drove off the ferry and drowned in the river. She overheard, but in her family she knew: *never* ask questions. Granny cried so loudly that it frightened her. When Dorothy saw Grandpa in his coffin, she thought he was asleep. She wanted to wake him up so Granny would quit crying.

These are sweet little stories, and we want to encourage this behavior to a certain extent. But like everything else in life, such behavior carried to excess represents problems. Children may believe they are responsible for another's feelings. That implies guilt. Children may assume an adult role of caretaker. That robs them of their ability to be children. Carried to excess, trying to be good can lead to adult dysfunction. In dysfunctional families we send a clear message: "Don't talk; don't trust; don't feel."

## Isn't It Good to Be Good?

Fear of their own death, fear of God's wrath, or fear that another loved one will die produces our "perfect" children. Trying to be good is a good thing, but these fears also produce children with severe personal problems. No one can always be that good.

It is good to be real. When we try to be so perfect that God won't punish us, we won't die, and no one will want to abandon us, we actually push people away. Holding on too tightly is another form of pretending the hurt isn't there. No one can be *that* good all the time, so when we have naughty thoughts or behaviors, we stifle them. Our naughtiness goes inside. We may even, for a while, successfully hide it from our-

✛══════════

*It is good to be real.*

══════════✛

selves. We can also hide from God behind a mask of good works.

Then as we live life, we see signs of our imperfection. We see it when we kick the dog and wonder what brought that on. We see it when we yell at the grocery clerk and think, *Where did that come from?* When our anger and fear go inside, they hurt us. When we don't express these emotions toward the person who needs to hear or to God, they come out in little spurts of anger directed toward innocent recipients.

We see these fears played out in those who

- become angry if their best friend befriends another; they can have only one friend at a time.
- are "everybody's" best friend.
- leave us feeling exhausted because they seem to suck our energy away.
- boss us around without cause or compassion.
- try to control our behavior.
- never get upset or angry, never disagree with us.

Jeff and I could never argue. Every time that mother pointy finger headed his way, his little eyes would glaze over and a feigned smile would cover his face. It didn't matter what I said; he was in another world. Communication ceased. We learned how to argue by having him spend some time alone writing out his gripe list. I would have him write out why he was angry with me, Dad, his friends, his teammates, his teachers—anyone in his life. He would then make a list of what needed to change in our relationship. He and I could talk emphatically with the finger pointed at the sheet of paper. When I moved from the paper to him, the fake smile would appear and the eyes would glaze over. He was gone!

## What Do We Do with Our Bad Behavior?

One of the greatest tragedies that comes from this fear-laced goodness is that our children never learn about the healing act of confession and the freedom of forgiveness.

Reuben Welch says it best in his book *We Really Do Need to Listen:*

*If we pray only our holy prayers
our unholy thoughts remain unholy still
and pace the cage, feeding on our fantasies
and daydreams.
And sometimes
they grow strong enough
to break out and wreak havoc!
Then a holy person can do an unholy thing
And we wonder:
How can that be?
It is because the unacceptable thoughts and
hungers and
desires and
yearnings
were not truly opened up to God for his
renewing,
cleansing,
healing grace!*

*Whatever you desire, don't define it beforehand. Pour it all out to God, and his Spirit will define and edit and cleanse.*[15]

Reactions to grief are healthy. They show that a child is smart enough to know that what is happening is not good. Grief reactions become problems only when they are destructive, when they are not outgrown or overcome with time, or when they are turned inward. Our job is not to prevent reactions but to help meet children's needs during the reactive period so they will recover rather than become trapped in a destructive cycle.

> *Our job is not to prevent grief reactions but to help meet children's needs during the reactive period so they will recover rather than become trapped in a destructive cycle.*

*It seems I have spent a lot of time in a daydream state. It has been a safe haven for me when I haven't been ready to deal with heavy things in my life. I remember a few times, as I was growing up, when people would ask me questions about Dad or if I had brothers and sisters. I would quickly switch over to this dream world and tell them that my dad had some job where he had to travel a lot, such as an airplane pilot. I would sometimes not even really address the part about brothers or sisters. It really made me feel uncomfortable.*

*Likewise, a lot of the children I work with deal with their anger and frustration at coming from an abusive home by creating a fantasy world for themselves. They have created it out of necessity. It is a safe place for them to be. My fantasy world was a place where I didn't have to worry about brothers dying, dads leaving, or life being life. It seems to be a natural way for most children to deal with huge disasters in their life until they are at a developmental point at which they can deal with life's hard knocks.*

*As I grew older, I started slowly easing out of my fantasy and was able to look at the pain in my life as a real part of it and cope. This was in a large part due to my high school youth pastor being of great help to me. His advice was simply to start telling people the truth, even if it was only one person at a time.*

*Still, even today I need time to hide in my dreams. But I also know that I need to come back and address life before it gets out of control.*

*Parents, remember that all children are naughty sometimes. If your children seem too good to be true, they probably aren't. They need to be assured that you will always love them. They also need freedom to go inside to a daydream world for a while, if they need to.*

## Part 5

# The Ultimate Question: Why?

For a long time it seemed as though a little black cloud followed me wherever I went. Four deaths, one of them my infant son. A senseless divorce from a man I adored. A move from my life in Fresno, California, a life I loved, in order to be near family (whom I also loved) because I needed their support. An unwelcome career change. A little boy whose life was forever altered and, I feared, damaged beyond repair. People would try to cheer me up. They would say, "You know, God's going to use this to help others someday."

I would respond bitterly—and yes, I meant it: "Oh, that's wonderful. I've prayed all my life that I could be someone's bad example."

At least now I know I was in good company. In the aftermath of his wife's death, C. S. Lewis wrote A Grief Observed. He was honest with his pain—so honest, in fact, that he originally published it under a pseudonym, perhaps because he was embarrassed to be a leader in the Christian church and have such deep negative emotions. Grief is selfish and irrational, whether you're six or sixty!

And at least now I know that God is bigger than my circumstances and able to grow good from even the toughest soil—a bitter, broken heart.

It is the ultimate question, the question that haunts the minds of both parents and children, the question that doesn't really have an answer, but the question we all cry out when grief strikes: Why would a good God let this happen?

*God is bigger than my circumstances and able to grow good from even the toughest soil—a bitter, broken heart.*

No two deaths are alike. No two circumstances are alike. Some of you are facing such horrendous grief and circumstances that reading this was just a little Band-Aid on your broken, bleeding hearts. Some of you who read this will be overwhelmed by the greatness of my loss; some will think it melodramatic. People have asked me if in hindsight it was really that bad. My honest answer: Yes. It was far worse than words can convey. Yes . . . but God is good. When I faced that horrible year, I honestly believed it would destroy me. Now I have perspective. It was a huge, destructive hailstorm in an otherwise very blessed life.

---

*A child's natural question to everything is, "Why?" I remember asking my mom and others in my family, "Why did Justin have to die?" Those I asked would weep some and say, "I don't know, Jeff" and hug me. I'm glad they didn't try to give me answers. I'm glad they gave me a hug.*

*I really don't know how to deal with the question of why. There just isn't any answer ever good enough to justify any tragedy that happens in life. I have learned to realize that indeed life is short, and life sometimes hurts. What keeps me going is my constant desire to be around those who care about me, to enjoy their company, to find fun things in life to do, and to do them. I don't ever want to look back on life and say to myself, Well, I wish I had . . .*

*Just take care of what you need to. Don't let sorrow rob you of the joy that is available. I don't like watching the news anymore. I don't want the news to sap the joy right out of me. Find what you love to do and do it, even if your life is in pieces. Doing what makes me happy has helped get me through the hardest times in life.*

## Chapter 22

# Why Would a Good God Allow This to Happen?

*W*ith Justin life was a series of highs and lows. One day the doctors would tell us he could live his life in a vegetative state; the next, "Anything's possible. He could be normal." He improved and made so many strides in spite of the odds. One day I shared with a friend what God was doing in his life. I told her, "It looks as though God is going to heal him."

She replied, "Of course God will heal him. He's already shown you that. You've got to start praising him now that the work has been done. Not to praise him ties the hands of God."

When she left, I fell to my knees in prayer, guilty of murder. I sobbed, "God, is my lack of faith preventing you from working a miracle in the life of my own son?"

God responded with Scripture: "It is by grace you have been saved, through faith—and this [faith] not from yourselves, it is the gift of God" (Ephesians 2:8). As real as if it had been audible, God said, "When I want you to praise me for Justin's healing, you won't be able to keep your mouth shut. But until then you are not to try to play God or to manipulate me through praise."

---

There is no answer to the why question—at least not in the concrete terms that we humans seek. But there is hope.

## What Causes Us to Question God?

As we develop our philosophy of life and suffering, as we pass our heritage of faith on to our children, life's dichotomies confront us with our shallow beliefs, our yo-yo emotions, and our sometimes selfish actions. The following circumstances especially frustrate us.

*When you cannot mourn what was, you must mourn what might have been.*

### Deifying the One Who Died

You may have become a new member in the family of a person who died and had no faults. That's a problem! *Everyone* has faults. If we create the impression that he or she was perfect, we give our children a skewed picture of life. When the deceased was a parent, a stepparent who is human can never measure up. When the deceased was a sibling, the remaining child can't be perfect. Life will be impossible.

God always demands that we walk in truth. When we shortchange truth, we create severe emotional problems in our children. Share both the goodness and the humanity of the one who died. Make the memory real.

### Telling the Truth When It's Tough

It is difficult to face the death of one you love who loved you in return. It is gut wrenching to face the death of one who abandoned you, who never returned your love, or who abused you. It is a different kind of gut wrenching to face the death of one who took his or her own life. What do you do then?

When you cannot mourn what was, you must mourn what might have been. That's harder. You need to reach forgiveness and closure. To do that, you must own your anger.

We can write a letter to the deceased, an honest letter, a letter mixed with love, hate, anger, and tears. I wrote one to my father, who abandoned me before I was born. I wrote it over thirty years after his death. An excerpt reads, "A part of me loves you, and a part of me hates you. I'm sorry, God, but that's the truth."

Until we reach closure on our grief, it robs us of our today. Strange as it seems, I had carried my anger and grief, very buried, for a lifetime. Once I owned it and expressed it, I could forgive my dad. That's freedom.

### Compounded Losses

Losses are compounded when many difficult things occur at once:

"Because of the death, we lost our home."
"Mom died; Dad couldn't handle it, so he left us."
"Dad died; Mom remarried an awful person within six months. In a way I lost them both. Losing Mom was harder because she had a choice."
"When Dad died, Mom abused me."

Usually when we have compounded losses, we need both counseling and grief support groups. So do our children.

### Surrogate Parenting

Some of you have legally adopted children who have lost their parents. Some of you are mentors or surrogate parents to children who have informally adopted you. Sometimes both parents died; sometimes one parent died and the other ran away. What will you tell the children? How will you deal with your own feelings of inadequacy? How can you be a parent while you keep another parent's memory alive?

Remember that the age-appropriate truth, however painful, is always your powerful ally. Remember that every child needs a parent, and because of life's circumstances, that's you. Do what you would want another person to do if he or she were the surrogate parent to your biological children.

### Handling Your Anger

You may be legitimately angry with the deceased. Perhaps the person overdosed or committed suicide or did something else just as foolish. Now you are involved in the lives of his or her children as a caretaker, either formally or informally. What do you do?

You must own your anger, deal with it in a healthy way, and control it as you comfort the children. Remember that a child's self-image is closely tied to both parents, living or dead, and to you as their caretaker. Anything negative you say about their parents, even when it's true, hurts the children you love. Tell the children the truth without placing your bitterness in the middle. Admit your anger, but calmly explain why you feel that way; they are probably angry, too.

### When It Seems God Doesn't Care

There are times when life just doesn't make sense. He was studying to be a minister; he had devoted his life to God. Why would God take him home? Missionaries were killed, leaving small children. Where was God?

We will never be able to answer these questions; we can only lead the children involved to the God who can comfort them. We may never know why, this side of eternity. When we can help our children learn who God is and who and Whose they are, they don't really need to know why. We can remind them that this too shall pass.

I am reminded constantly that however short and however futile, life is precious. This was by God's design, not by an accident of fate. It is because of our ability to bond so deeply with others that we are able to comprehend a little bit how much God must love us. Our why questions will never be answered. Our who, what, and what now questions must be!

## What Helps Us When We Don't Know Why?

As we struggle with these thoughts, there are some truths and life principles we must embrace.

*God is the author of goodness.* The evil, the sin, the death, the disease that cause us grief are permitted by God because he chose to give us a free will. If he hadn't, we would be robots. We need to constantly remind ourselves that everything God created was good. When Adam sinned and death entered the world, God had already enacted Plan Jesus. He is a God of redemption. God does not send evil into our lives, but he is bigger than anything that can happen to us.

> *Our why questions will never be answered. Our who, what, and what now questions must be!*

*Grief and sin are not synonymous.* So often when we go through periods of grief, our friends are like Job's friends. They insist that our sin has caused our misfortune. When troubles visit our homes, we should certainly talk to God and ask if there is sin we need to take care of. But we cannot get caught in the trap that says we have the power to bring good or evil upon ourselves. That is a lie of the Enemy. We need only look as far as Hebrews 11 to see that faith and circumstances don't necessarily match.

*God is worthy of our praise regardless of our circumstances.* This is a difficult concept because so many people attempt to manipulate

God through praise. Some would attempt to tell us that our lack of faith or our inability to praise have caused our losses. Some urge us to praise God for everything. Scripture tells us instead to praise God in everything. We can always find something to praise God for! He gives us strength when our strength is gone. He gives us peace when it doesn't make sense. He walks with us when our heart is broken and we must cry our tears. He gives us health. Wow! The list is endless.

*Heaven will be worth whatever price we have to pay.* The Bible tells us that we can't even imagine what heaven will be like. I don't want to miss it! Whatever I must face here is nothing when I catch a glimpse of the glory of God.

Years remove the freshness of grief for a child, just as they do for an adult. But years don't erase a child's love or memories— just as they could never erase my mother love. Loss is a natural part of living. Losing his brother at the age of three forced Jeff to face death much earlier than he should have—but I wish you could know my son, so full of compassion! The loss has not destroyed him; it has helped to define him.

When trials come, we must teach our children, through our example, that there is a heaven and that it is worth striving for. In intensity, death affects a child as it does all of us—our hurt will equal the extent of our involvement. We must allow children to hurt, without shame, in their own way.

Perhaps rather than helping children forget, we should help them build a heritage in heaven. Our Justin is one of our many treasures who live there now. Maybe—who knows?—maybe someday your child, like Jeff, will say, "I choose to go to heaven. After all, I have a brother there waiting for me."

And to know that both my sons will be there is worth whatever price I have to pay.

*We are never alone.* Hebrews 11 is the great chapter on faith. It speaks of those who have gone before us to show us the way to heaven. Chapter 12 speaks of them as being a great cloud of witnesses as we run our race of life. It gives me great comfort to know that Justin sits in my heavenly grandstands. When I'm discouraged, I can imagine him saying, "Hey, Mom, you can do it!"

That is also the hope I endeavored to plant in Jeff's heart. When trials confront him and when he is weary and thinking of giving up, I want him to hear a little voice from heaven saying, "Hey, Bro, get up and try again! You don't want to miss out on this adventure!"

*Death is a part of God's plan of redemption.* Death was not God's great failure because Adam sinned. It was instead God's great grace and creativity at work on the plan of redemption. He knew we humans couldn't understand unconditional love. He knew we would forget about heaven in the midst of our daily lives. He knew we couldn't quite grasp love for one we have not seen, so he created a plan that included death. He sent Christ to show us that there is life after death and that we can live eternally with him. Then he planted those we love in heaven so we would miss them and long to see them. Someday I'll see Mama and Gram and Daboy. I can hardly wait. There's also a little boy there. Nothing on earth could keep me from that reunion. I know the pain of empty mother arms.

The Bible tells me that God's arms are empty and that he longs for me when I stray. It will be far more wonderful, beyond my wildest dreams, incomprehensible, when I see Jesus. That's where I want to spend my eternity!

---

*The great reunion of family and friends. It will one day happen in heaven. Oh, what a party it will be! At that given moment in which we enter eternity, all the grief and sadness my mother and I experienced when my brother died will no longer be there. We will be with God and my brother for eternity.*

*Just think of the happiness you feel when you see a long-lost friend. That to me is a very happy moment. The happiness I feel when I see friends I haven't seen in a while will be nothing compared with what God has prepared for me when he allows me to be reunited with old friends and family who have gone before me.*

*That is what helps get me through a lot of what life brings. Life isn't easy. God is good and will provide what is sufficient to meet our needs each day as they come. For me the hardest thing to do is to allow people to help when I'm struggling and hurting. It is also the best thing I can let happen. Please let yourselves be helped when life is hard.*

# Afterthoughts

*W*riting is a soul-searching experience. When I write about certain memories, I cry again. I relive the moment of pain and the moment of failure. I mourn those things I did wrong as a parent—and *every* parent does so many wrong things!

I like to read pearls of wisdom. Those that follow have become so much a part of me that I have forgotten in most cases who said them. They are not original, though. They came from a multitude of friends and sages who paved my path so I could love life again.

- The joy and the pain constantly coexist, and that's okay.
- Playing the victim is not okay.
- Hurt now or hurt later. Hurts don't die if you bury them.
- Hope really is eternal.
- A baby is God's opinion that the world should go on.
- Parenting mistakes are never fatal as long as you remember the words and actions to "I'm sorry; I love you, and I will always love you."
- Wherever you are in the grief process, it's okay to be there. It's not okay to stay.

There are also pearls of wisdom we pass on to our children. We speak them in both actions and words:

- Plan as though you will live forever. Live as though each day were your last.
- Life is a daily series of choices. Make better choices today than you did yesterday.
- Bad behavior has consequences.
- Never forget that we're playing on the same team, you and I.
- We won't get over this, but we will get through it—together!

Parenting—it's tough! God was the first parent. Adam and Eve didn't obey him, either; but *everything* he created was good. He even had a plan when Adam and Eve sinned and death entered our world. That plan was—and is—heaven.

So as we strive to answer our children's myriad questions, let's look to God's principles:

- Tell the truth.
- Listen more than you talk.
- Remember grace.
- Forgiven doesn't mean forgotten.
- Love never fails.
- A good story is worth a thousand scoldings.
- Love breeds love.
- Heaven is real.
- We can be happy for others and sad for us at the same time.
- God is the author of goodness. He didn't cause our sorrow.
- God did allow it.

- God will grow good from it.
- We may never know why. We don't need to when we know Who.

Along with the many things I am learning about parenting, I continue to be amazed at the parenting skills of God. One of my favorite promises is found in Isaiah.

> *When you pass through the waters,*
>   *I will be with you;*
> *and when you pass through the rivers,*
>   *they will not sweep over you.*
> *When you walk through the fire,*
>   *you will not be burned;*
>   *the flames will not set you ablaze.*
> *For I am the LORD, your God,*
>   *the Holy One of Israel, your Savior. . . .*
> *You are precious and honored in my sight,*
>   *and . . . I love you.*
>
> ISAIAH 43:2–4

What a great blueprint Isaiah gives us parents!

- When you cry, I will hold you.
- When you are sad, I will cry with you.
- When you need to talk, I will listen.
- When you need a friend, I'll be there.
- When you need correction, I'll hold your hand.
- You *will* make it through, and you'll be stronger.
- You're mine, and I will always love you.
- Even when I enter eternity, you will draw strength from my memory.
- Death is not the end; it is a beginning.

# Resources

$\mathcal{I}$n the aftermath of his son's death, my friend Fred searched local bookstores and called support groups to find comfort. I bought him two of my favorite books and loaned him about thirty books, with notes attached, from my personal library. He consumed them and continued his search, adding information about his favorites to my collection. His passionate quest for comfort typifies the grieving world. One caller told me she had read fifty-six books; a participant in my Divorce and Grief Recovery program reported having read over one hundred. Grief is a consuming pastime.

When I published my first book, *Justin, Heaven's Baby*, I thought I was writing only to Christian audiences, but everyone wants to know how anyone faces loss and crisis. For this reason, I am providing a short annotated list of what I have found to be powerful books or resources in my own life. What helped me may be one little piece in your puzzle of healing. I have learned, though, that God is a God of personal relationships. What touched my heart may help you, but he will tailor your own healing—and he will tailor the healing of each of your children. You're his child, not just an acquaintance. You can call him Daddy, and his lap is big enough to hold you, whether you are four or forty.

I hope you find comfort from these sources. Some are new; some were written many years ago, but they speak to me as though they were written to me personally, just yesterday.

———

Bayly, Joseph. *The Last Thing We Talk About*. Elgin, Ill.: Lifejourney, 1992. Originally published as *The View from a Hearse*. Elgin, Ill.: David C. Cook, 1969.

Joseph Bayly lost three of his children to death; one in infancy, one in childhood, and one as a teenager. This is tender and poignant. I keep going back to reread it; he always speaks peace to my broken heart. Over the years I have given it to dozens of grieving friends. The newer books are good but this one's a classic.

———. *Psalms of My Life*. Wheaton, Ill.: Tyndale House, 1972.

This book features modern-day psalms. I've quoted them often; we read "A Psalm in Children's Hospital" at Justin's memorial service. You may be able to find only a used copy, but it's well worth tracking down.

Benson, Bob. *Come Share the Being*. Hendersonville, Tenn.: Deeper Life Press, 2000. See *www.deeperlife.org*.

Philosopher and parent extraordinaire, Bob Benson reminds us of the joys of raising children. This is a sweet book for parents seeking a relationship with God that impacts our daily lives and influences our children to live for Jesus.

Bramblett, John. *When Good-bye Is Forever: Learning to Live Again After the Loss of a Child*. New York: Ballantine, 1991.

This has been recommended by several of my friends.

Brown, Elizabeth. *Sunrise Tomorrow: Coping with a Child's Death*. Old Tappan, N.J.: Revell, 1988.

Many of my friends have found great comfort from this book.

Colgrove, Melba, Harold N. Bloomfield, and Peter McWilliams. *How to Survive the Loss of a Love.* Los Angeles: Prelude, 1991.
This is a classic work on grief. It is written to the person who is in the stage of shock and cannot follow the theme of a book written from cover to cover. Although its primary audience is the divorced adult, it provides a blueprint for mourning any loss.

Graham, Billy. *Hope for the Troubled Heart.* Dallas: Word, 1991.
In typical Billy Graham fashion, this book helps us merge the realities of life's heartaches with the goodness of God. It helps us shape our philosophy of life.

Heavilin, Marilyn. *Roses in December.* Eugene, Ore.: Harvest House, 1998.
Marilyn Heavilin has a writing and speaking ministry in the area of grief recovery that blends insight from the loss of a son and from her work as a high school counselor. Her work is accurate, faith-filled, and heartwarming.

James, Diana. *Bounce Back.* Camp Hill, Penn.: Christian, 1997.
Diana James has background and expertise in grief/loss recovery and in working with children. She has an audiotape, *Helping Children Cope with Loss.* She can be reached at 393 W. Willowbrook Drive, Meridian, ID 83642.

Kübler-Ross, Elizabeth. *On Death and Dying.* New York: Simon and Schuster, 1997.
Dr. Kübler-Ross conducted the landmark research on grief. She identified the typical stages a person in mourning experiences.

Lewis, C. S. *A Grief Observed.* New York, Bantam, 1976.
Recently the subject of the feature film *Shadowlands,* this is a must-read book for those who need help putting words to their tears and doubts.

Littauer, Florence. *Personality Plus.* Old Tappan, N.J.: Power, 1983.
Florence Littauer touched my own mourning mother-heart. She
lost two sons in infancy. Her teaching on personalities has become
foundational to my work with high-risk youth.

Florence's daughter Marita Littauer, through an organization
called CLASSSpeakers (*www.classervices.com*), offers a wealth of
resources on a variety of topics. She also speaks and publishes widely
on personality types, and books speakers for group activities.

Marshall Lockett, Sharon. *Justin, Heaven's Baby.* Kansas City, Mo.:
Beacon Hill, 1983.

————. *Surviving Separation and Divorce.* Grand Rapids: Baker,
1988.

————. *When a Friend Gets a Divorce, What Can You Do?* Grand
Rapids: Baker, 1990.

Marshall-Lockett, Sharon. *Crisis, Grief, and Loss . . . and How to Help
Your Students Through It.* Laguna Niguel, Calif.: Educational
Innovations, 2001.

————. *Smarter, Not Harder!* Albuquerque: Classervices, 1997. See
*www.score-ed.com.*
My books are all available through my web site: *home.earthlink.net/
~sharonmarjo.*

O'Conner, Joey. *Heaven's Not a Crying Place.* Old Tappan, N.J.:
Revell, 1997.
This informative resource shares how to teach your children about
death and dying.

Rando, Therese A. *How to Go On Living When Someone You Love Dies.*
New York: Bantam, 1991.
This book comes highly recommended by those in fresh grief. It is
well written, insightful, and comforting.

Rawlings, Maurice. *Before Death Comes.* New York: Bantam, 1991.
  An emergency room cardiologist, Dr. Rawlings became a Christian by observing dying patients. His work clearly describes afterlife experiences, as observed from his lifesaving position in the emergency room, both of those prepared to meet Jesus and of those who are not ready. His work is poignant, interesting, and inspirational.

Schuller, Robert H. *Life's Not Fair, but God Is Good.* Nashville: Nelson, 1991.
  In typical Schuller style, this book helps readers trust God with their lives in tough times, knowing that he is always at work to redeem heartaches. It is especially helpful in formulating a philosophy of grieving.

Smith, Harold Ivan. *A Decembered Grief.* Kansas City, Mo.: Beacon Hill, 1999.
  Harold Ivan Smith has written, spoken, and researched extensively on grief. He is a member of the Association for Death Education and Counseling and the National Hospice Association's Council of Professionals. This particular book provides pragmatic and healing help for those anniversary celebrations that are a constant reminder of our loss.

---

*Churches.* Many churches host grief and/or divorce and grief recovery programs for adults. I am available to consult with those wishing to establish a program and needing resources. Many larger churches hold programs to support children through loss. The Crystal Cathedral uses the program Confident Kids, a ministry of Family Ministries International, Inc. Their web site is *www.confidentkids.com.*

*Community directories.* Your local library carries community directories that provide the names, addresses, and phone numbers of local organizations that can help you deal with any problem. A section contains resources for grief recovery.

*Hospitals.* Many hospitals hold grief recovery classes. My first experience in this field was a class offered through Veterans Hospital in Fresno, California. It changed my life. Every hospital has chaplains and social workers. Call your local hospital to ask for resources and classes.

*Hotlines.* Many organizations and churches have hotlines for you to call when you are in crisis. Your telephone directory will list those in your area. Guide your children carefully in this endeavor, since both helpful and hurtful sources are available. The Crystal Cathedral in Garden Grove, California, has hotlines that are manned twenty-four hours a day: 714-NEW-HOPE for adults and 714-NEW-TEEN for teens.

*Internet.* New resources and chat rooms are added daily. To find the latest help in grief, search for the combined keywords grief plus children. You will need to be careful editors, however, since you will find diverse worldwide viewpoints. Even young children can find chat rooms. Since they can get both helpful and hurtful advice this way, make sure you share with them in this experience. This is a good time to teach them how to make wise choices about what they put into their minds.

*Mortuaries.* All mortuaries provide handouts to assist with the grief process. Most mortuaries also provide referrals; many offer grief recovery classes.

*Organizations.* A number of organizations support those experiencing grief and loss. Consult Internet directories, telephone directories, and community directories for those near you. Contact the National Association of Christians in Recovery (*www.christianrecovery.com* or 714-529-6227) for a list of Christian resources in your area.

*Schools.* Many schools host support groups to help children deal with grief. If your local school does not have one, SCORE (*www.score-ed.com*) can help them set one up.

# Notes

1. Phil Southerland, speaking as leader of the divorce and grief recovery program at Evangelical Free Church, Fullerton, Calif., 1981.

2. Benson, Bob, *Come Share the Being* (Hendersonville, Tenn.: Deeper Life Press, 2000), 67–68. See *www.deeper.life.org.*

3. Dick Innes, director of Acts, International, speaking at the divorce and grief recovery program at Crystal Cathedral, Garden Grove, Calif., April 25, 2001.

4. Robert H. Schuller, *Life's Not Fair, but God Is Good* (Nashville: Nelson, 1991).

5. Billy Graham, *Angels* (Dallas: Word, 1975), 167–68.

6. The Choir, "Clouds, " from *Chase the Kangaroo,* (Waco, Tex.: Myrrh, 1988), compact disc.

7. David Heller, *Dear God: Children's Letters to God* (New York: Doubleday, 1987), 14.

8. Florence Littauer, *Personality Plus* (Old Tappan, N.J.: Power/Revell, 1983).

9. Stuart Hample and Eric Marshall, *Children's Letters to God: The New Collection* (New York: Workman, 1991), 14.

10. Joseph Bayly, *The Last Thing We Talk About* (Elgin, Ill.: Lifejourney/David C. Cook, 1992), 106.

11. Art Linkletter, interview by Robert H. Schuller for *The Hour of Power*, Crystal Cathedral, Garden Grove, Calif., August 13, 2000.

12. The Academy of Child and Adolescent Psychiatry, *www.aacap.org* and *mentalhelp.net/factsfam/suicide.htm.*

13. Robert H. Schuller, interviewing Art Linkletter for *The Hour of Power*, Crystal Cathedral, Garden Grove, Calif., August 13, 2000.

14. Hazel Lee, delivering the keynote address at the women's retreat, College Church of the Nazarene, Bourbannais, Ill., 1986.

15. Reuben Welch, *We Really Do Need to Listen* (Nashville: Impact/John T. Benson, 1978), 81–82.